# Multicultural Perspectives in Music Education

## Volume Two

## Third Edition

Edited by
William M. Anderson and Patricia Shehan Campbell

Published in partnership with
MENC: The National Association for Music Education

ROWMAN & LITTLEFIELD EDUCATION
A division of

ROWMAN & LITTLEFIELD PUBLISHERS, INC.
Lanham • New York • Toronto • Plymouth, UK

Published in partnership with MENC: The National Association for Music Education

Published by Rowman & Littlefield Education
A division of Rowman & Littlefield Publishers, Inc.
A wholly owned subsidiary of The Rowman & Littlefield Publishing Group, Inc.
4501 Forbes Boulevard, Suite 200, Lanham, Maryland 20706
http://www.rowmaneducation.com

Estover Road, Plymouth PL6 7PY, United Kingdom

British Library Cataloguing in Publication Information Available

**Library of Congress Cataloging-in-Publication Data**

Multicultural perspectives in music education / edited by William M. Anderson and Patricia Shehan Campbell.—3rd ed.
  p. cm.
 "Published in partnership with MENC: The National Association for Music Education."
Includes bibliographical references and index.
 ISBN 978-1-60709-539-2 (cloth : alk. paper)—ISBN 978-1-60709-540-8 (pbk. : alk. paper)—ISBN 978-1-60709-541-5 (electronic)—ISBN 978-1-60709-542-2 (cloth; v. 2 : alk. paper)—ISBN 978-1-60709-543-9 (paper; v. 2 : alk. paper)—ISBN 978-1-60709-544-6 (electronic; v. 2)—ISBN 978-1-60709-545-3 (cloth; v. 3 : alk. paper)—ISBN 978-1-60709-546-0 (paper; v. 3 : alk. paper)—ISBN 978-1-60709-547-7 (electronic; v. 3)
 1. World music—Instruction and study. 2. Multicultural education. 3. Music—Instruction and study. I. Anderson, William M. II. Campbell, Patricia Shehan.
 MT1.M93 2010
 780.71′073—dc22

2009031558

∞™ The paper used in this publication meets the minimum requirements of American National Standard for Information Sciences—Permanence of Paper for Printed Library Materials, ANSI/NISO Z39.48-1992. Printed in the United States of America

# Contents

# Foreword

I congratulate the editors of and contributors to this expanded third edition of *Multicultural Perspectives in Music Education* and urge readers to learn from the authors' expertise and experience and apply them in their classrooms. Shortly after the publication of the first edition, MENC: The National Association for Music Education, the Society for Ethnomusicology (SEM), and the Smithsonian Institution collaborated in a symposium on multicultural approaches to music education. We hoped the synergy of MENC's expertise in classroom teaching, SEM's expertise in the study of many musical traditions in their cultural contexts, and the Smithsonian's experience in the presentation of a variety of musical traditions to the general public would contribute in concrete ways to the development of materials for classroom teachers. Since then, these three organizations have continued their efforts to increase the diversity of musical traditions experienced in U.S. music education. This third edition features contributions from many new authors, boasts a larger three-volume format, directs readers to online resources undreamed of in 1996, and displays an even greater inclusivity of genres and cultural perspectives than its predecessors.

North America has been multicultural since the American Indians spread throughout its vast extent, speaking a variety of languages, creating a multitude of cultures, and exchanging objects, ideas, and musical practices with one another. The creation of the United States out of English colonies, French territories, Spanish settlements, and Native American nations resulted in a multilingual and multicultural nation that has been subsequently nourished by millions of immigrants. Today, even small towns may be ethnically and culturally diverse; large cities have long been so. Sometimes viewed negatively, sometimes positively, the cultural heterogeneity of the United States presents a challenge to its entire population that can best be met through education and experience from preschool onward.

Contemporary music is already multicultural; it is our music education that remains predominantly Eurocentric. Whether one scans the radio dial, delves deeply into iTunes or other online music sources, examines the work of early twenty-first-century American composers of concert music, or posts compositions online, one discovers a creative mixture of musical styles that draws on many different traditions and processes. Our students come from many different traditions, wear clothes made in many different countries, eat food from many different cuisines, and have families with roots in many different places. Just as spicy salsa has joined ketchup as a national condiment of choice, so have Caribbean-born reggae, Afro-pop, Indian film music, and hundreds of other genres found a place in the entertainment centers of American homes as well as in myriad headphones and car stereos. As the authors of this volume argue, we must address this new reality in our classrooms, our ethnomusicological theory, our exhibits, and our publications.

Not every member of an ethnic or cultural group will prefer the music, cuisine, and culture of his or her ancestors. For example, some European Americans may choose to dine on Chinese food and dance to Caribbean music, while some immigrants from Asia and the Caribbean may prefer fast food from McDonald's and heavy metal music or French cuisine and nineteenth-century European classical music. The exposure to a variety of traditions is, however, a central part of education for the twenty-first century, a century certain to be filled with complex cultural choices and increasing international and intercultural interdependence.

This expanded third edition of *Multicultural Perspectives in Music Education* goes much further than its predecessors in providing materials to assist music teachers in modifying their classes and involving their students in new forms of music making and new understandings about sounds. The fourteen-year-old second edition has undergone major updates and improvements, and the authors and MENC are to be congratulated on this new publication. I hope it will be read with care, used with imagination, and received by all with surprise, enthusiasm, and enjoyment.

Anthony Seeger
Professor of Ethnomusicology, UCLA
Director Emeritus, Smithsonian Folkways Recordings
Former president of the Society for Ethnomusicology
and the International Council for Traditional Music

# Preface

*William M. Anderson and Patricia Shehan Campbell*

Music in American schools has been historically associated with the art and traditional musics of Western Europe, with its harmonic functions, transmission systems, and notational heritage. Despite the presence of American Indians long before (as well as during) the formative years of the republic, the arrival of Africans beginning in the seventeenth century, and the waves of immigrants from Europe, Latin America, and the Asia-Pacific region since the 1840s, the K–12 music curriculum has seldom reflected the ethnic diversity of American society. Rather, the schools have been a bastion for teaching European-styled choral and instrumental music, with European-styled pedagogical approaches. Students of every color and creed have been more likely to learn music that is Germanic rather than Japanese, French rather than Filipino, and Irish rather than Iranian-Persian or Asian-Indian.

The American colonial heritage was linked to Western civilization by nature of those Europeans who first settled the eastern seaboard. The pervading sociopolitical system is an extension of Anglo-Saxon and Germanic traditions, and yet today's American society has emerged as a unique blend of cultures from every part of the world. It is no longer fitting or relevant to the interests and needs of American schoolchildren to maintain a too-narrow focus on the customs and values of a single culture in the social sciences and the arts; such an approach ignores the realities of our multicultural society. Further, in this increasingly international age, schools must engender broad understanding of people from every part of the globe. Cultures and countries are increasingly interdependent in economic and political matters. Our survival as a world community may depend on our ability to understand the similarities that bind us and the differences that distinguish us as subsets of the human species.

MENC: The National Association for Music Education maintains the slogan "Music for *every* child—every child *for* music" as the core of its professional philosophy. Embedded in this slogan is the knowledge that school music must be more broadly defined to encompass the ethnic diversity of American schools and society. Beginning with Karl W. Gehrkens's recommendation in 1924 that music instruction be available to all children, a gradual awakening of interest in music of other cultures has been evident.

The Tanglewood Symposium of 1967 paid particular tribute to the importance of musics of various ethnic and racial groups, triggering the first substantial movement of music educators in the direction of multicultural music education. By the 1970s, MENC had established a Minority Concerns Commission, followed by a Multicultural Awareness Commission, with the intention of raising the level of consciousness and promoting the use of traditional musics of many cultures in the curriculum. The growing interest among music educators in world musics has been evident in the large numbers of workshops at national, regional, and state conferences and in special issues of the *Music Educators Journal*. The 1990 Washington, D.C., Pre-Conference Symposium on Multicultural Approaches to Music Education, presented under the auspices of MENC's Society for General Music, the Society for Ethnomusicology, and the Smithsonian Institution, was a seminal event in urging the development of broadly based multicultural curricula in music at all educational events.

As definitions of equity, pedagogy, and multiculturalism were established in the 1990s,[1] they began to flood curriculum guides, methods books, and national and local mandates. Within many American universities, especially where no ethnomusicologist appeared on faculty, a single course in "world music" emerged. There were at this time, in a small number of progressive university programs, a few gamelans and "African" drumming ensembles, an occasional steel drum band (more likely in the percussion department) or gospel choir (more often through student services or African American Studies programs), and the cameo appearance of southern African, East European, and Pacific Islander songs within the repertoire of choral groups. A mere fifteen years ago, "multiculturalism" was still emerging as a buzz word in university-wide curricular designs and required courses. The drive toward cultural diversity in music education was on at universities, and prospective teachers were shifting into a broader repertoire of music to perform, listen to, and imagine as curricular possibilities in their future teaching.[2]

Teaching resources, however, have not developed fast enough for those who are philosophically convinced of the merits of multicultural teaching in music. Nor are they comprehensive or global in scope: emphasis has been on certain percussion styles of West Africa, East (but not Southeast) Asia, and the Caribbean (but not the Andes); children's songs from many lands; and recently on Mexican mariachi bands in secondary schools. Still, music teachers have been left largely to their own imaginative devices, to their own extended efforts to design lessons from random resources, and to summers spent reading scholarly writings on the music traditions of unfamiliar cultures. The commitment to providing students with global perspectives in music involved a considerable time expenditure for those few teachers who translated, interpreted, and finally applied the results of independent research to their classrooms.

The Society for Ethnomusicology has continued to develop ways to infuse world musics into collegiate, secondary, and elementary school programs. Beginning with philosophical statements that provided a rationale for world musics, the Society established an Education Committee to review appropriate curricular materials and to provide workshops for educators at their national conferences. These efforts lessened the gap between research in the field and the dissemination of world musics to the general public. With the continued development of educational technologies, an earnest effort by some ethnomusicologists committed to teaching and learning led to such digital projects as the Smithsonian Folkways' website, the Associate for Cultural Equity, and EVIA (Ethnomusicological Video for Instruction and Analysis). These projects are indicative of scholars' response to the needs of teachers to create rich learning experiences in music and culture.

The third edition of *Multicultural Perspectives in Music Education* represents the twenty-first anniversary of this landmark book. Like its predecessors, the third edition is a compendium of descriptions of the world's musical cultures supported with lessons for elementary and secondary school general music classes. These lessons give music teachers the practical means to integrate world music traditions into the school curriculum. There are singing games for young children in the primary and intermediate grades, a sampling of unison and multipart songs for secondary school choral ensembles, and percussion (and other instrument ensemble) pieces of varying levels of complexity for students in every music educational context. Far beyond the scope of the first and second editions, the third edition significantly expands the spectrum of musical cultures with new lessons in every chapter, along with newly developed chapters on jazz and rock and world beat. Especially noteworthy are lessons based on downloadable resources so that teachers can easily acquire needed materials. As before, this book serves a dual purpose in reinforcing the knowledge of music elements through their use and interpretation in various musical styles and the development of a greater understanding of people in other cultures. The contributions of music educators and ethnomusicologists come together in this volume, ensuring that music examples are both representative and realistic for teaching in the schools.

Finally, we would like to thank the principal contributors, as well as the publications staffs of Rowman & Littlefield Education and MENC: The National Association for Music Education for their assistance in producing this new edition.

## NOTES

1. James A. Banks, "Multicultural Education: Historical Development, Dimensions, and Practice," in *Handbook on Research in Multicultural Education*, 2nd ed., ed. James A. Banks and Cheryl McGee Banks (San Francisco: Jossey-Bass, 2004), 3–29.
2. Patricia Shehan Campbell, *Teaching Music Globally* (New York: Oxford University Press, 2004).

# 1

# Teaching Music from a Multicultural Perspective

*William M. Anderson and Patricia Shehan Campbell*

A multicultural approach to learning necessitates organizing educational experiences for students that develop sensitivity, understanding, and respect for people from a broad spectrum of ethnic-cultural backgrounds.[1] If students are to learn from a multicultural perspective, teachers must develop an educational philosophy that recognizes the many cultural contributions made by different peoples. That philosophy centers on developing an understanding that there are many different but equally valid forms of cultural expression, and encourages students to develop a broad perspective based on an understanding of, and a tolerance for, a variety of opinions and approaches.

Multicultural music education reflects the cultural diversity of the world in general and of the United States in particular by promoting a music curriculum that includes songs, choral works, instrumental selections, and listening experiences representative of a wide array of ethnic-cultures. It also encourages the interdisciplinary study of different cultural groups through not only music but also art, dance, drama, literature, poetry, and social studies. Performances by choral and instrumental ensembles, as well as stories told by storytellers, dramatic presentations, puppet shows, and folk dances, are some of the experiences that enliven classroom study based on a multicultural curriculum. The ultimate challenge in multicultural music education is to provide avenues of exploration so that students can gain a better understanding of the world and of their American heritage.

A multicultural approach to music learning in American schools is important for many reasons. For one thing, the United States is comprised of an extremely diverse population, with people from more than one hundred world cultures residing here. Many ethnic groups now number in the tens of thousands, and some in the millions. Major changes in the patterns of immigration to this country have occurred in the four centuries since the founding of Jamestown, Virginia, in 1607, when Native Americans and a few Europeans were the only cultural groups. Initially, the largest number of immigrants came to the new world of America from European countries, first from northwestern Europe and then from southeastern Europe. Substantial numbers of people from the African continent, especially the western region, from such nations now known as Ghana, Nigeria, Dahomey, Guinea, Liberia, Sierra Leone, and the Ivory Coast, also arrived during the eighteenth and nineteenth centuries. During the nineteenth century Asians, initially primarily Chinese, also began to arrive in substantial numbers, and throughout the twentieth century numerous people from many areas of Asia, particularly India and Japan, emigrated to the United States. By the latter part of the twentieth century, Koreans, Filipinos, Vietnamese, and the Khmer of Cambodia and the Lao of Laos were further diversifying the Asian American population. Pacific Islanders have joined U.S. communities as well, especially in California, Oregon, Washington, Utah, and, of course, Hawaii. More recently, the primary influx of immigrants to the United States has come from Latin America. While the European stream of immigrants has slowed to a trickle, and Native Americans proudly continue their traditions but in reduced numbers, the American population has continued to expand into a rich mosaic of many hues and views. It is estimated that as the U.S. population, which is currently approximately 307 million, grows to approximately 400 million by 2050, half of this growth will occur among immigrants or their children.[2] By 2050, the population distribution of the United States is projected to be 10 percent Asian and Pacific Islanders, 16 percent black, 22 percent Latino, and 52 percent of European heritage.[3]

Many geographical areas throughout the United States now have very ethnically diverse populations, with populations of some of the groups represented increasing at dramatic rates in recent years. Major metropolitan regions identify themselves as "cities of nations," but ethnic-cultural diversity is also found in many smaller communities throughout the country. At one time it was fashionable to speak of America's cultural diversity in terms of a "melting pot," but this has been superseded by the analogy of a "patchwork quilt" in which various ethnic communities contribute to the national culture as they maintain distinct identities. While English is the lingua franca of the nation, Americans uniformly uphold the dream of democracy that allows for freedom of speech, freedom of religion, and the right to vote—freedoms that allow for shades of ethnic-cultural difference between both individuals and families. Thus, American communities can be microcosms of the world while also holding to commonly held beliefs of social justice and civil equity in institutions such as schools.

The dynamics of cultural diversity are reflected at all levels in American schools with increasingly ethnically and linguistically diverse student bodies. School curricula in all subject areas are now being designed to encourage broad cultural perspectives, and administrators and faculties are placing increased emphasis on designing curricula that help students develop an understanding of the cultural diversity of both their world and their own country. The former helps students develop international perspectives that will prepare them to live in a global environment; the latter focuses on the very nature of the United States itself, a country composed of a large variety of different cultures that must understand each other and work together for the common good of the nation.

Five dimensions of multicultural education, proposed by leading multicultural educator James Banks (2004), are influential in curricular design and delivery in American elementary and secondary schools today. *Content integration* directs teachers to the use of examples and content from a variety of cultures in teaching key concepts. *Knowledge construction* suggests that teachers help students understand how cultural assumptions and biases within a discipline influence the ways in which knowledge is constructed within it. *Prejudice reduction* focuses on the racial attitudes of students and how they can be modified by teaching methods and materials. *Equity pedagogy* is an important means by which teachers modify their teaching in ways that facilitate the academic achievement of students from diverse racial, cultural, and social-class groups (including differentiating teaching styles to suit student learning styles). Finally, the creation of an *empowering school culture and social structure* is central, so that the tracking, grouping, and labeling of students are reconsidered and abandoned, in order that a school culture that empowers students from diverse racial, ethnic, and cultural groups can be formed.[4]

In music, a multicultural approach to education is clearly in keeping with what is perhaps the most significant trend of the past half century: the growing understanding of music as a global phenomenon in which there are a number of highly sophisticated musical traditions based on different but equally logical principles. In essence, students must be taught the operative principles of each musical system in order to understand it. Clearly, school systems must ensure that music curricula contain balanced programs that are representative of the world and also of the multicultural nature of the United States itself. Such an approach is a fair and equitable practice, one that provides teachers with the wherewithal to provide occasions for their students to experience firsthand the principles of content integration, knowledge construction, prejudice reduction, equity pedagogy, and an empowering school culture and social structure.

Many teachers are now aware of the need to present a broad spectrum of music to their students. MENC: The National Association for Music Education has given priority attention to the multicultural mandate through conference sessions, symposia, and a number of publications, including this three-volume book series, devoted to introducing students to a variety of musical traditions from throughout the world and the United States itself. A number of other national and international organizations, including the Society for Ethnomusicology, the National Association of Schools of Music, and the International Society for Music Education, have strongly endorsed the study of world musics at all levels of instruction. Specialized pedagogical methods such as Kodály and Orff-Schulwerk embrace musical diversity and feature some of the world's musical traditions in their annual conference programs and publications. The National Standards for Arts (Music) Education particularly stress the importance of multicultural perspectives in commenting that all students should sing, play instruments, and listen to music from diverse cultures; such a statement supports both musical and cultural diversity within music classrooms, running from early childhood through high school bands, choirs, and orchestras.[5]

Responding to this multicultural mandate, music teachers at all levels have broadened their perspectives. General music teachers are developing both cross-cultural and culture-specific musical units of study (often in collaboration with classroom teachers), and band, choral, and orchestral programs include an increasing number of arrangements, transcriptions, and newly composed pieces in particular "world music" styles. There has also been considerable growth of traditional music ensembles both in and outside of schools, including world music drumming ensembles, marimba groups, mariachi, steel-pan ensembles, jazz groups, gospel groups, Latin American dance-music groups of various kinds, and Asian ensembles such as the Filipino kulintang ensembles in Seattle, Washington, and the Firebird Youth Chinese Orchestra of San Jose, California.

To support the increasing interest in multicultural approaches to music education, domestic and international book and digital-media companies are producing a wide variety of materials on music cultures of the world. Teachers are working with culture bearers to prepare "authentic" notations and recordings to accompany them, and a number of small companies are producing teaching packets for presenting different musical traditions. Music series textbooks for elementary and secondary schools now embrace a broadened music curriculum based on examples from a wide variety of music cultures. The highly regarded Smithsonian Institution has developed an online "tools for teachers" component, so that its considerable archive of American-heritage and world music selections can be accessed and applied to classrooms of children and youth. It seems clear that studying music from a multicultural perspective has become an integral part of music instruction at all educational levels in schools of the United States, as well as schools in a number of other areas of the world.

## BENEFITS OF MULTICULTURAL APPROACHES TO MUSIC EDUCATION

There are many benefits from a multicultural approach to music education. Although many people have encouraged an investigation of world musics as a way to promote intercultural and interracial understanding, multicultural music study can also provide a number of strictly musical benefits. First, when students are introduced to a great variety of musical sounds from all over the world, their palette of musical experiences is expanded, as they come to realize the extraordinary variety of sonic events worldwide. It is particularly important to note that an early exposure to a large array of musical sounds is essential in helping students become receptive to all types of musical expression.

Second, students begin to understand that many areas of the world express music that is as sophisticated as their own. Historically, peoples of both Western and non-Western cultures often believed that Euro-American classical music was "superior" to other musics. Today, composers, performers, and teachers have come to realize that many equally sophisticated music cultures are found throughout the globe and that Western classical music is just one of the many varied (and often complex) musical styles.

Third, students can discover many different but equally valid ways to construct music. For many students this may be one of the most important benefits derived from a study of music in its multicultural manifestations. Even young children can discover that music from a given culture may have principles that differ significantly from those of their own musical culture, and that one must learn the distinctive, inherent logic of each type of music. What would be an unacceptable practice in Western music may be perfectly acceptable in music from another area of the world. Further, it is clear that the terminology used for Western music often is not appropriate for describing another musical tradition, where more global-oriented nomenclature is called for.

Fourth, by studying a variety of world musics, students develop greater musical flexibility, termed by some as "polymusicality." They increase their ability to perform, listen intelligently to, and appreciate many types of music. Some teachers find that when students gain a positive attitude toward one "foreign" music and are able to perform and listen intelligently to that music, they become more flexible in their attitudes toward other unfamiliar musics. Through their involvement with other musics, students develop a number of vocal and instrumental techniques. Their capacity for learning different musics grows, and they are able to study and perform new musics with increased understanding and ease. Further, with this flexibility, they are much less prone to judge a new music (whether Western or non-Western) without first trying to understand it. In addition, by studying the function of such elements as melody, rhythm, texture, timbre, dynamics, and form in producing various musics, students begin to reappraise Western music and often come to view it in a completely different manner. In essence, when students study a variety of musics, they become more aware of aspects of their own music that they have previously taken for granted.

## APPROACHES TO ORGANIZING A MULTICULTURAL MUSIC CURRICULUM

Music specialists, working in conjunction with classroom teachers and subject specialists, can develop curricula for the study of a number of music cultures, both from the world at large and from the United States. While there are a number of approaches, music teachers may wish to consider organizing study units around cultural groups highlighted in the social studies curricula at each grade level. At the elementary level, for example, musical study for these units may include singing songs, making and playing instruments, improvisation, movement or dance, and focused listening. And, in conjunction with the art teacher, students may also study visual art examples from the culture currently under study, while the physical education teacher may provide assistance with dance and other movement exercises. Classroom teachers, especially those specializing in social studies and language arts, bring other dimensions to the study of different cultures by having students read folktales, poetry, and other literature; produce dramatic productions; view DVDs; search Internet sites; and write reports. These experiences help students learn not only the history and geography of another people but also the unique ways in which music and other art forms are expressive of that culture.

While young children are in the early stages of their musical development, upper elementary, middle school, and secondary school students are at a pivotal point in their development of skills, knowledge, and attitudes toward music. They possess the coordination and strength needed for performing vocally or on instruments. They can think in abstract, critical, and analytical ways. They are often intrigued by the new and unfamiliar and may be fascinated by a comparison of "new" to "known" phenomena. These students have the potential to examine musical cultures beyond their immediate surroundings. They do not easily change their preference for their own music, but they may explore with enthusiasm various musics through active participation.

In addition to gaining a more global perspective, students can learn that many musical styles of the world are represented in the United States. This nation of immigrants provides ample opportunities for discovering the music, literary and visual arts, cuisine, and various customs of different cultural groups. Students who experience a variety of what now constitute "American musics" will gain a new understanding of the cultural plurality of their country. The study of this plurality has become an important curricular theme in the upper elementary grades and in secondary schools nationwide.

There are a variety of ways in which music teachers may organize curricula to broaden musical study for their students.

## Music Concepts

A music curriculum based on multicultural musical experiences can focus on the study of the fundamental concepts of music. A musical concept's chart can be made on the chalkboard, on a poster board, or as a bulletin board; and as students learn a new music through performance experiences and directed listening, they are asked to "fill in" information on distinctive aspects of melody, rhythm, timbre, texture, dynamics, and form. Organizing musical study in terms of a concepts chart provides an effective way of summarizing how distinctive treatments of various musical concepts define a particular musical style. It also allows students to focus on contrasts among different musical styles, which leads to an understanding that there are many different but equally logical ways to construct musical sounds.

## Performance

Multicultural music study can be approached through various performance experiences in singing, playing instruments, and moving to music. Through performance, students become actively involved in experientially discovering how musics of various cultures are constructed. The pedagogical principles of Emile Jaques-Dalcroze, Zoltán Kodály, and Carl Orff provide teachers with excellent models for designing multicultural musical experiences. Choral performances can just as likely feature a multipart song from Bulgaria or South Africa as something from the repertoire of Bach or Brahms—and middle and high school choristers can sing these songs with the nuances that are characteristic of the particular stylistic traditions. Band and string ensembles can play suitable arrangements of music from Russia and Romania, Bolivia, Brazil, and Benin. In addition, the musical skills of teachers, developed through many years of ear training, conducting, and applied lessons, are invaluable in the engagement of students in music-making experiences.

From preschool and the primary years onward, children can learn to sing songs that represent numerous cultures. These songs can be taught authentically, and certainly in the original languages. Children enjoy learning to pronounce new words, and they may best identify with the culture and people by using a song's original language. In secondary school choral ensembles, students are capable of performing multipart pieces with sensitivity to the nuances of both music and language. Their performances can be further enhanced by the addition of gestures and movement associated with the vocal tradition. Teachers need not use harmonic piano accompaniments when they do not resemble the practice of the original cultures (unless they are striving for a culturally distant musical arrangement rather than a culturally close musical experience); many traditional songs may be most accurately performed without accompaniment or with basic rhythmic patterns.

In addition to singing, students can also learn to play musical instruments from various cultures. Indigenous instruments from many areas of the world are now available in the United States and can be used effectively in schools. For example, a school can purchase an African *mbira* (plucked idiophone), *shekere* (gourd rattle with a netted covering of beads), *marimba* (wood xylophone with resonators), *djembe* (single-headed conical drum), and *agogo* (pair of iron bells). These instruments, or replicas of them, are effective in teaching students about musical heritages from sub-Saharan Africa. Likewise, xylophones are central when playing traditional music from Cambodia to Zimbabwe, and they can be easily played by both young and older students. Other percussion ensembles, including those from West African, Caribbean, Latin American, and Chinese cultures, can be organized to perform important drum- and gong-based traditional music that uses available classroom instruments. In school systems that do not have access to authentic musical instruments from various cultures, teachers can frequently create instruments that simulate the appearances and sounds of real instruments. By coordinating performance on handmade instruments with media presentations (projected digital images, DVDs, etc.) that show the original instruments, teachers can provide effective and valid presentations of different musical cultures.

People from other areas of the world perform their own native musics in many areas of the United States. This is particularly true in urban areas and in college and university communities in which there are distinguished performers from many different cultures. Such artist-musicians, often referred to as *culture bearers* or *tradition bearers*, provide an important resource for teachers and schools, and many are willing to instruct and perform.

Along with singing and playing instruments, students can experience various musical traditions through dancing and other movement to music. Movement activities can center on developing an understanding of basic concepts such as rhythm and form. Students move to the beat, meter, rhythmic patterns, and tempo changes in music. They also learn to "feel" the form in a work by devising movement activities to illustrate different sections. Students can also experience different musics by learning the folk dances of these traditions. Because of the close relationship between motor activity and mental activity, movement is likely to facilitate and enhance conceptual learning. In music learning, the mind and body function together, and the sensory feedback from movement is connected to higher mental processes. Children create natural and spontaneous rhythms when they listen to music; these movements provide the impetus for expressive movement and patterned folk dance.

### Guided Listening

Concurrently with experiencing the fundamental structural principles of other musics through performance, students are ready to listen perceptively to recorded performances of world musics. Listening to examples of many different musical cultures is an important component of any instructional program. A large number of recordings from most areas of the world are now available in the United States, and, as exemplified in this book, many selections on the Internet are easily available from downloadable sites. Further, many excellent examples of world musics also appear on DVDs that have the obvious advantage, for example, of providing both the sound and sight of musical instruments being played. Finally, a number of performing artists from other countries now live in the United States, and others come to visit this country each year. Thus, teachers can have actual performances in their classrooms. Such presentations are especially effective in helping children identify with the cultures from which the music is derived.

### Integrated Learning

Developing a cultural context for featured musical pieces or styles is an important part of a multicultural music program. Although students can explore other musics without investigating the cultures themselves, the most effective approach coordinates a study of the people and their music. Students enjoy learning about different peoples from both their own and other countries by studying unfamiliar customs, crafts, paintings, sculptures, architecture, literature, music, and dance. Through an interrelated study of many aspects of a culture, students develop new and important understandings of other peoples, and they begin to realize the inherent place of music and the arts in other cultures.

## THE DESIGN OF THE THIRD EDITION

The third edition of *Multicultural Perspectives in Music Education* is organized in three volumes that include information and suggestions for teaching students many world musical heritages. Volume 1 includes the music of sub-Saharan Africa, African American music, music of Latin America and the Caribbean, and jazz and rock. Volume 2 encompasses the music of Europe, European American music, music of native peoples of North America, and music of Oceania and the Pacific; it concludes with a chapter entitled "World Beat." Finally, the third volume focuses on the music of East Asia, Southeast Asia, South Asia, and the Middle East.

This book is designed as a practical, experience-oriented guide for helping students develop a broad understanding of musics in their world and an appreciation of their multicultural musical heritage in the United States. The lessons are intended to serve as launches, to be adapted and developed by teachers for individual school settings. In this way, the book is a stimulus to a teacher's own creative curriculum. It focuses on helping students discover some of the inherently different but equally valid ways in which various cultural groups organize musical events. Finally, this book is intended to help students learn to understand and appreciate music as something that fulfills a worldwide human need for artistic expression, and something that is personally and socially meaningful.

## NOTES

1. While some people differentiate between *multicultural* and *multiethnic,* we refer here to ethnic-culture and leave other cultural considerations (such as age, gender, religious affiliation, and lifestyle) beyond the scope of this discussion. See James A. Banks and Cheryl McGee Banks, *Handbook of Research on Multicultural Education* (San Francisco: Jossey-Bass, 2004). For a half century of efforts in multiculturalizing music education, descriptive phrases have run parallel to *multicultural music education,* including *world music education, intercultural education, global musics in education, world music pedagogy,* and *cultural diversity in music education.* While nations, communities, and institutions select their preferred vocabulary, these varied terms intersect at the point of sensitivity to, and respect for, cultural communities and their views and values.

2. *Time,* October 30, 2006, 8, 41–54.

3. *Time,* December 2, 1993, 14. While projections are just that, it is noteworthy that the demographic profile for the United States is indeed changing. While the 1990 census notes that 8.5 percent of Americans are of Spanish/Hispanic/Latino origin, in 2010 this population had increased to 15.1 percent (www.census.gov/population/www/projections/index.html).

4. James A. Banks, "Multicultural Education: Historical Development, Dimensions, and Practice," in *Handbook of Research on Multicultural Education,* 2nd ed., ed. James A. Banks and Cheryl McGee Banks (San Francisco: Jossey-Bass, 2004), 3–29.

5. Consortium of National Arts Education Associations, *National Standards for Arts Education: Dance, Music, Theater, Visual Arts* (Reston, Va.: MENC, 1994), 26–29, 42–45.

# 2

## Music of Europe

*Patricia Shehan Campbell*

Think "Europe" and splendorous images may come to mind, emanating from travel brochures, and photos and video footage of personal trips and professional tours, and the artifacts and stories of family and friends who have lived there.[1] Conjure up these images: the Eiffel Tower in Paris, St. Peter's Cathedral in Rome, and London's Big Ben clock tower; boats on the Rhine or Danube rivers, the breathtaking Alps of Switzerland, the Côte d'Azur of southern France, the islands of Greece, and the fjords of Norway; European sidewalk cafes, galleries of great art, the music of concert halls and opera houses, and exquisite cuisine. These are classic European images. But consider these scenes as well: shepherds and their flocks against the backdrop of rocky hills; village women en route to the central market for fresh vegetables, fruits, and grains; three-day rural wedding feasts and their great spreads of food and drink and dancing; churches with onion-shaped towers rather than spires and steeples; farms where sickles, scythes, and motorized combines work together. Such are the images of the "other Europe," the more ancient European cultural stratum still found in the rural areas and in the countries in the eastern regions.

Europe is a land of great diversity, a conglomerate of many images and many nations. Viewed as a whole, Europe is perceived as the foundation of Western civilization. The now widespread Western traditions of governance, education, and the arts first developed in Europe, and European contributions to world progress continue today. Over the centuries, Greece, Italy, Spain, France, Germany, and other nations have emerged as world leaders in the arts, the humanities, and the sciences. The European Union emerged in 1993 to encompass twenty-seven members (as well as others waiting to join), allowing a common trade policy, a shared vision of foreign politics, and a standardized system of laws—even as distinctive regional cultures are maintained from one nation to the next.

The continent of Europe is approximately the same size as the United States, including Alaska. It is outranked in size by all other continents except Australia, but it embraces a great diversity of climates, natural resources, and densities of population. Europe extends from the icy Arctic Circle in northern Scandinavia to the temperate climate of the Mediterranean countries of Spain, Italy, and Greece. The British Isles are its farthest western countries (beyond which is the Atlantic Ocean), and its eastern borders are flanked by the Asian continent and areas of the Black and Caspian seas. Europe is in close proximity to major cultural regions including North Africa and the Middle East. Despite a one-time history of isolationism, cultural exchanges among countries have allowed for fascinating new cultural manifestations. Immigrants from Africa, the Middle East, Asia, and Latin America are further diversifying the European nations.

European peoples vary in ethnic composition, language, and religion. For its size, Europe is the most polyglot area in the world. Celtic, Romance, Teutonic, Baltic, Slavonic, Hellenic, Turkic, and Finno-Ugric are some of the broad language classifications, which can be further distinguished by country or region. The Romance languages, for example, include Italian, French, Spanish, Portuguese, and Romanian, as well as Walloon (Belgium), Catalán and Galician (Spain), and Ladin (Italy). Another language group is Slavic, which can be classified into three groups according to regions in Eastern Europe; for example, South Slavic alone is divided into six language groups. Is it any surprise that language has fostered national consciousness and political divisions throughout the continent?

Although there are similarities among European peoples, the cultural regions are distinctive in many ways. Some divide the continent along political boundaries, but the physical characteristics of the land itself may provide clearer borders between cultural regions. England, Ireland, Scotland, Wales, and Northern Ireland developed customs different from those of the mainland because of their somewhat remote island status. Three of the four Scandinavian countries—Norway, Sweden, and Finland—are separated from the continent by the Baltic Sea; their Nordic cultures are more similar to one another than to the rest of Europe.

The Mediterranean countries of Spain, Italy, and Greece share a more moderate climate than that of central Europe, and their cultural influences include North Africa and the Middle East. (The editors have placed Turkey, while sometimes included in this grouping, in the chapter on the Middle East, on the basis of cultural, political, and economic factors.) The Germanic countries of Austria, parts of Switzerland, Germany itself, and the Netherlands are united by language and location in the western portion of Europe, and the Alpine regions of the first three countries contribute similar customs beyond their political borders. Eastern European countries, including Poland, the Czech Republic, Slovakia, Hungary, Romania, Bulgaria, Russia, Ukraine, Albania, and the smaller nations east of the Adriatic (Bosnia-Herzegovina, Croatia, Macedonia, Montenegro, Serbia, and Slovenia) remained agrarian societies well into the twentieth century; the rustic peasant life of this region still exists in many communities. The "Romantic-Atlantic" countries of France, Portugal, and Belgium, which complete the list of major European countries, are akin in location (all are coastal countries on the Atlantic) and language (from the Romance family).

The splendors of Europe are at hand, whether through the romance of transcontinental travel, staring out the windows of the great railway cars that link the cities and the villages, or through the more immediately accessible avenues of knowledge: the literature and the fine arts. Study of these cultural contributions is likely to lead to a deep understanding of Europe's people, and such study may just as surely transport the learner to this historical land of so many of our forefathers. In particular, a view of the music and the dance of these countries offers insight into both the diversity and the similarities among the people of Europe.

## CHARACTERISTICS OF EUROPEAN MUSICS

As languages differ among ethnic groups, so do music styles. European traditional music can be divided into two genres: songs and dance music. Although some may view the traditional music (sometimes interchangeably called folk music) of Europe as a single unit with common elements maintained across the continent, each region, country, and community has its own style, songs, and dances. Since all music consists of fundamental sonic elements (melody, rhythm, texture, form, and timbre), these are the elements evaluated when reviewing the styles of Europe as a whole and those of the six distinctive regions studied in this chapter: the British Isles, Scandinavia, Germanic Western Europe, the Atlantic-Romantic countries, the Mediterranean, and Eastern Europe.

European traditional music has many unifying elements. Although we immediately hear differences between the musics of Sweden and Italy, they resemble each other far more than either one resembles Chinese or Native American music. What is so characteristic about European folk music?

Song structure is one important element of European music. Across the continent, the use of strophic form is widespread: melodies are sung more than once with different words for each repetition. The verse-by-verse and verse-chorus organization of songs reinforces the view of Europe as a distinct musical unit.

Meter is another facet common to European traditional music. Most songs and dance music are metric, so there is a regular and consistent recurrence in the accent patterns. Duple and triple meters (and even irregular meters such as 5/8 and 7/8) feature the repetition of accents in a cyclic manner. In songs, this meter is usually linked to the poetry. Music with no obvious metric pattern is rare in Europe.

Certain song genres are found in many parts of Europe. These include the narrative song, love songs, ceremonial songs, seasonal songs, and dance music. Song stories called ballads and their lengthier cousin, the epic, are prominent throughout the continent. Clearly, then, European music can be efficiently classified as songs and dance music.

There are instruments that are associated with the music of the various European countries, but several are so predominant throughout the continent that they can be referred to as pan-European instruments. There are perhaps three such instruments: the fiddle, the accordion, and the bagpipe. Although they vary in construction, size, and shape, their tone quality and principles for sound production do not. Other common European instruments include flutes, drums of various types, plucked lutes, and zithers. Certain instruments that are less widespread, including the Swiss alphorn, the double reeds of the Mediterranean countries, and the Irish tin whistle, provide a means of distinguishing the music of a country or region.

## THE WESTERN ISLES

Folk music in the British Isles (or more appropriately "the Western Isles") of England, Scotland, Wales, and Ireland (and Northern Ireland) is somewhat related to the art music of Western Europe, even though the British Isles are geographically separate from the continent. Folk songs, ballads, and dance tunes, like so many madrigals and art songs, are commonly organized into four phrase melodies or four-line stanzas in duple or triple meters. Folk music of the British Isles has retained its modal structure to a greater extent than has folk music on the continent. The vocal melodies range from strictly syllabic English ballads to the Irish Gaelic lyrical and melismatic songs of love and war. In fact, Irish music is essentially melodic, relying on ornamentation rather than harmony for its effects. Traditional instruments of the British Isles include fiddles, bagpipes, flutes, and harps. The following elements characterize music and songs in the British Isles:

Melody: Based in C, A, D, and G modes (Ionian, Aeolian, Dorian, and Mixolydian); syllabic vocal music in Britain, more decorative and ornamental music in Ireland

Rhythm: Duple and triple meter; jigs in 6/8, 9/8 ("slip jig"), and 12/8; reels and slow hornpipes in duple meter

Texture: Homophonic song (melody and chords) in Britain; heterophonic music in Ireland, in which several pitched instruments may play simultaneous variations on the melody

Form: Many two part binary folk songs (AB)

Genres: Jigs, reels, ballads, and love songs

Timbre: Fiddle, flute, tin whistle, Scottish highland bagpipe, smaller uilleann "elbow" bagpipe of Ireland, Irish bodhran (flat drum), Celtic harp, and concertina

## SCANDINAVIA

Denmark, Sweden, Norway, and Finland are referred to jointly as Scandinavia. Denmark, Sweden, and Norway share common linguistic elements, and Sweden, Norway, and Finland sit side by side, extending from the Arctic Circle into the Baltic Sea. Scandinavian folk music has been influenced by the cultivated traditions of Germany, and the villages maintain traits of an ancient musical tradition. The parallel fifths, or organum, of medieval church practice appear in the folk music of nearby Iceland. Only Albania shows similar early forms, probably because both areas were isolated from Europe's cultural mainstream for centuries. Modal folk tunes and major and minor melodies are prevalent. Stringed instruments, including the standard fiddle and the Norwegian hardanger fiddle, the Swedish nyckelharpa, the Finnish psaltery called kantele, and Scandinavian dulcimers, are frequently played to accompany songs and dances. Typical Scandinavian songs display the following elements:

Melody: Based in major, or mixing major and minor modes; arpeggios and triad-like figures

Rhythm: Duple and triple meter (including dances such as the vals, hambo, and polska); meter obscured by overlapping measures in much instrumental music

Texture: Homophonic (chordal) or polyphonic (independent and interwoven melodic lines)

Form: AB (binary) and ABA (ternary) forms

Genres: Dance music and love songs

Timbre: Fiddle (usually played in pairs or larger ensembles), hardanger fiddle (Norway), kantele psaltery (Finland), dulcimer, nyckelharpa, and flute

## GERMANIC WESTERN EUROPE

The rich folk music traditions in the Germanic countries of Western Europe faded rapidly by the nineteenth century, when other forms, such as church and school songs, easy art and community songs, and popular hits and ballroom dances, grew in popularity. Music making had once been nurtured, but the industrialization of this region created a void of social functions including seasonal agrarian customs and gatherings for spinning, corn husking, and other communal activities. Of the remaining folk songs of Germany, Austria, Switzerland, and the Netherlands, the most common consist of arpeggiated melodies set in major keys and in duple or triple time.

Strophic forms, a simple syllabic style, and elementary harmonic sequences characterize the music. In the alpine regions, there is a distinctive song style called jodler, whose melodies contain wide-ranging leaps and are cast in a major key. Germanic peoples who still use folkloric styles live in the mountainous regions of the area and share instruments like the alphorn, the accordion, the wooden hammered dulcimer, and the zither. Folk music of the Germanic countries generally follows these guidelines:

Melody: Songs mostly in major keys; triads and sixths used frequently in melodies
Rhythm: Duple and triple meter, with an emphasis on triple time in southern Germany (Bavaria), Switzerland, and Austria
Texture: Homophonic, melody with chordal accompaniment; polyphonic song tradition
Form: Variety, with emphasis on AB (binary) and ABA (ternary)
Genres: Ballad, love song, jodler
Timbre: Alphorn (Switzerland), accordion, wooden hammered dulcimer, zither, occasional brass band, or rommel pot (Dutch friction drum)

## ROMANTIC-ATLANTIC EUROPE

France, Portugal, and Belgium are "Romantic-Atlantic" countries because they are coastal countries on the Atlantic and because their people speak languages of the Romance family. Of course, there are other countries that border the Atlantic Ocean, and there are other Romance-language nations; these three countries, however, share both geographic and linguistic elements. Folk songs in these countries are largely monodic and sung as solos. Chants and rounds are associated with the carnival days preceding Lent, "begging songs" with Christmas, and egg-rolling songs with Eastertide. There are songs whose rhythms and incantations arise directly from work such as wood carving, shepherding, and spinning. Typical instrumental sonorities in this region include the drone of bagpipes, the grinding timbres of the hurdy-gurdies, and the noisy strains of village wind bands. Belgium also shares in the Germanic tradition, just as Portuguese music frequently sounds Spanish in flavor.

Melody: Mostly major melodies, both diatonic and pentatonic; often conjunct (stepwise)
Rhythm: Duple meter predominant; 6/8 in Brittany (France) and northern Portugal
Texture: Homophonic (melody and chordal accompaniment)
Form: AB (binary) and ABA (ternary) forms
Genres: Seasonal and love songs
Timbre: Bagpipe, hurdy-gurdy, pipe and drum, and concertina

## MEDITERRANEAN EUROPE

North Africans and Middle Easterners have contributed to the music and culture of the Mediterranean countries of Europe: Spain, Italy, and Greece. (See volume 3, chapter 5 for a lesson on music in Turkey.) Although these countries each make unique contributions to the world's music, there are elements that are similar among them. The florid melodies are unmistakably Mediterranean, as is the somewhat nasalized vocal timbre of the singers. Much of the music is metered, but there is also considerable use of the free and flexible rhythms associated with declamatory speech. When musicians play in ensemble, they frequently create simultaneous variations of the melody, particularly in Greece and in the southern portions of Spain and Italy. The world-famous genre of Spanish flamenco dance music exemplifies the passionate music of the Mediterranean. Among the instruments common in these countries are guitars or other types of plucked lutes (Greek oud and bouzouki), double-reeds, and percussion instruments such as castanets, spoons, tambourines, and rattles. Typical Mediterranean music makes use of these elements:

Melody: Frequent use of minor melodies, largely melismatic and decorative; augmented seconds
Rhythm: Occasionally free of meter; some use of irregular, yet isometric patterns including sevens and fives (5/8, 7/8, 11/8)
Texture: Heterophonic; polyphonic and chordal in northern Italy and Spain
Form: Through-composed, AB (binary) form
Genres: Love songs and dance music (in Spain, flamenco; in Italy, tarantella; in Greece, tsamiko)
Timbre: Lutes (guitar, Greek oud, bouzouki), double-reeds, bagpipes, percussion (especially idiophones)

## EASTERN EUROPE

Eastern Europe encompasses a large geographic area and numerous countries. From north to south, they are Poland, the Czech Republic and Slovakia, Hungary, Romania, Bulgaria, Albania, and the smaller nations east of the Adriatic once known collectively as Yugoslavia (Bosnia-Herzegovina, Croatia, Macedonia, Montenegro, Serbia, and Slovenia); Russia and Ukraine are farther east and part of the Asian continental land mass. Eastern Europe is much less influenced by art music than is the rest of Europe, and traditional music is still quite prevalent. Bulgaria, Albania, Romania, and the six nations of the former Republic of Yugoslavia, known collectively as the Balkans, share certain style traits with the Mediterranean countries: melismatic singing, heterophonic texture, and irregular or free meter. The pentatonic melodies used by Hungarians are evidence of an ancient layer of musical culture in which pitches are transposed up or down a fifth. Parts of Poland and the Czech Republic show Germanic influences in the music's major tonalities, duple and triple meters, and use of anacruses. The farther east one moves, the more one will hear folk songs in older church modes, asymmetrical meters, and performances in the great polyphonic tradition. The following are elements common to eastern European styles:

Melody: Major, minor and modal; syllabic in northern and melismatic in southern areas; gypsy scale (augmented seconds of the Balkans)

Rhythm: Duple and triple in northern areas; asymmetrical and nonmetric music in the Balkans, little use of anacrusis

Texture: Heterophony or melody and drone in the Balkans; rich polyphony in the north

Form: Through-composed common in the Balkans; also AB (binary) and ABA (ternary) throughout the region

Genres: Epics, wedding song cycles, love songs, dance music (Hungarian csardas, Polish polka, Bulgarian rachenitsa, and Romanian hora)

Timbre: Lutes (plucked tamburs and tamburitza ensembles of Croatia and Serbia), gaida bagpipes (Bulgaria and Macedonia), accordions, cimbaloms (hammered dulcimers of Hungary), flutes, fiddles, and hand drums

## LESSON 1

**National Standards**

- Singing, alone and with others, a varied repertoire of music
- Performing on instruments, alone and with others, a varied repertoire of music
- Listening to, analyzing, and describing music
- Improvising melodies, variations, and accompaniments
- Understanding music in relation to history and culture

**Objectives**

Students will:

1. sing a number of modes common to Irish songs;
2. sing the song "Leaving Erin" first without and then with the characteristic melismas in the melody;
3. accompany the song on guitar;
4. identify the historical significance of the song's text;
5. locate the British Isles and Ireland on a map;
6. listen to examples of Irish jigs and tap the underlying pulse of the music;
7. improvise jig rhythms, both vocally and on drums;
8. identify traditional Irish instruments.

**Materials**

1. Guitars
2. Hand drums
3. Recording: "The Session" by The Chieftains 8 (available from iTunes)
4. Film: *Ireland* and "Riverdance" (Eurovision Song Contest 1994 Dublin) (available on www.youtube.com)
5. Map of Europe

**Procedures**

1. Sing each of the four common modes of Irish music: Ionian (the diatonic mode on C), Aeolian (on A), Dorian (on D), and Mixolydian (on G). Have the students imitate you: rote learning is the most efficient means of teaching these modes. Repeat the modes a number of times, changing the rhythm of the scale from quarter notes, to eighth notes, to eighth-note triplets, to combined rhythm patterns in order to challenge the students while reinforcing the sound of the modes.
2. Sing the Irish traditional song "Leaving Erin" (see figure 2.1). Where there are triplets notated in the music, sing the circled pitch only (as a quarter note). Learn the additional verses:

> Oh son, I loved my native land with energy and pride,
> Until a blight came o'er my crops—my sheep, my cattle died;
> My rent and taxes were too high, I could not them redeem,
> And that's the cruel reason why I left old Skibbereen.
>
> And you were only two years old and feeble was your frame,
> I could not leave you with my friends, you bore your father's name,
> I wrapped you in my woolen coat, and in the night unseen,
> I heaved a sigh, and bade goodbye to dear old Skibbereen.
>
> Oh father dear, the day may come, when in answer to the call,
> Each Irishman, with feeling stern, will rally one and all;
> I'll be the man to lead the van beneath the flag so green,
> When loud and high we'll raise the cry: "Remember Skibbereen."

---

All lessons were contributed by Patricia Shehan Campbell.

**Figure 2.1 "Leaving Erin"**

3. Sing the song with the triplet figures added. Note the change from the rather syllabic setting of much of the melody to melismatic sections in which several pitches are sounded on one syllable. This is the typical Irish lyrical song style. The recording of "The Session" by The Chieftains 8 (available from iTunes) contains more florid melismas in an instrumental setting.

4. Discuss the meaning of the text. The song is popular in Ireland and in Irish American communities. The harshness of the potato famine in Ireland and the dissatisfactions of the Irish with British rule brought about the migration of many Irish men and women to the United States and Canada in the mid-nineteenth century.

5. Locate Ireland on the map of Europe and note its relationship to Britain. Point out the division of Ireland and Northern Ireland, which today is still ruled by the British.

6. Listen to "The Session" for the metric structure and for the use of traditional Celtic instruments. Define a session as an informal meeting of musicians to play traditional Celtic tunes, keeping the music alive by improvising on familiar melodies. Use the following outline as a listening guide:

   a. "Elizabeth Kelly's Delight," A

      9/8 jig
      flute

   b. "Fraher's Jig," B

      12/8 jig
      bagpipe, bodhran (large hand drum), fiddle

   c. "Elizabeth Kelly's Delight," A

      9/8 jig
      bagpipe, flute

   d. "Dinny's Delight," C

      12/8 jig
      fiddle, flute, bagpipe

   e. "Fraher's Jig," B

      12/8 jig
      fiddle, flute, bagpipe

   f. "Dinny's Delight," C

      12/8 jig
      bagpipe, flute

   g. "Elizabeth Kelly's Delight," A

      9/8 jig
      fiddle, flute, bagpipe

7. Listen again, leading students in keeping the pulse of the music. Call attention to the heterophonic texture, in which the fiddle, flute, and bagpipe play slight variations of the same melody simultaneously.

8. Use a hand drum to keep a basic pulse. Lead students in performing subdivisions of the beat vocally on a neutral syllable such as "dee," "nah," or a combination of vocables. Ask students to imitate the jig-like patterns in figure 2.2 immediately after you play them.

9. Encourage the vocal improvisation of jig rhythms. For example, allow each student to contribute a spontaneously invented rhythmic pattern of one or two measures in length, followed by the group's imitation of it. As a challenge, suggest a melodic improvisation in 9/8 and 12/8.

10. Listen again to "The Session" for the jig rhythms, and ask students to distinguish between 9/8 and 12/8 by patting the leg on the first pulse and clapping on the remaining two 9/8 or three 12/8 pulses.

11. Show the images of Ireland found on "Ireland," www.youtube.com, which is subtitled "Let's Travel to Ireland." There are not only still photos of towns, fields, coastal areas, shops, pubs, and islands, but also Irish musicians and dancers. The audio track features a pennywhistle, which is joined later by fiddle, guitar, and bodhran. A film featuring components of *Riverdance*, the music-and-dance phenomenon, is also available on www.youtube.com for sharing the traditional dance music.

**Figure 2.2   Jig rhythms**

## Assessment

1. Perform the song, "Leaving Erin," vocally and with guitars and hand drums.
2. Tap, pat, or play an assortment of jig rhythms.

**LESSON 2**

### National Standards

- Singing, alone and with others, a varied repertoire of music
- Performing on instruments, alone and with others, a varied repertoire of music
- Listening to, analyzing, and describing music
- Understanding music in relation to history and culture

### Objectives

Students will:

1. listen to the waltz tune "Waltz from Boda" played by two fiddles;
2. identify the arpeggiated melody as typical of Scandinavian folk music;
3. clap the waltz pulse;
4. dance a modified waltz step;
5. play "Swedish Tune" on classroom instruments;
6. locate Sweden and Scandinavia on a map of Europe.

### Materials

1. Recording: "Waltz from Boda" from *The Swedish Fiddlers, Music from the Gathering of Fiddlers at Delsbo* (available from iTunes)
2. "Vasen Street Live at StringNation 2007" (available from www.youtube.com)
3. Recorders
4. Autoharp
5. Map of Europe

### Procedures

1. Define waltz as a dance in triple meter that developed in the ballrooms and community halls of early nineteenth-century Europe, especially in Germany and the Scandinavian countries. The Swedes call it vals.
2. Have students listen to "Waltz from Boda" as played by a pair of fiddles. Keep the triple meter pulse through pat-clap-clap movements; since the dance moves so quickly, try also a pat-clap-hold gesture. Note the melodic leaps in the arpeggios, the complementary and interweaving melodies of the two fiddles, and the three themes (the third of which characteristically shifts between major and minor keys).
3. Learn a modified waltz step like the following: Form an inner circle and an outer circle with students in couples (not necessarily boy-girl; see figure 2.3).

   Warm up by practicing a "limp step," moving right-left, left-right, around a circle in order to feel the rhythmic pattern (as shown in figure 2.4):

   *Theme 1*

   *Section A:* Couples face each other, feet together, weight on left foot, step in place (as shown in figure 2.5).
     *Section B:* Couple holds hands, as shown in figure 2.6.
     Repeat sections A and B four times, for a total of thirty-two measures: AB, AB, AB, AB.

   *Theme 2*

   *Shoulder hold:* Dancers extend their arms and hold their partners' shoulders. They turn together in small circles with right-left, left-right steps. Repeat this step eight times for sixteen measures (as shown in figure 2.7).

   *Theme 3*

   Couples promenade forward in skater's position with right-left, left-right steps; repeat eight times for sixteen measures (as shown in figure 2.8).

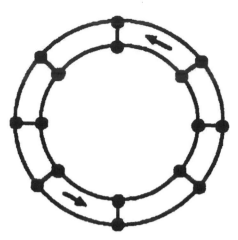

**Figure 2.3   Waltz inner-outer circle formation**

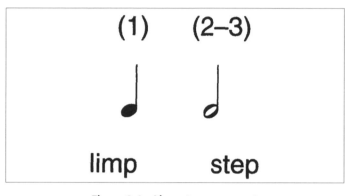

**Figure 2.4   Limp-step movement**

*Theme 4*

Couples separate, forming inner and outer circles. The inner circle moves forward and then back again; the outer circle moves backward, away from the circle, and back in. Repeat four times for sixteen measures (as shown in figure 2.9).

The form should go this way: Theme 1, 2, 3, 4; 1, 2, 3, 4; 1.

4. Lead the students in playing "Swedish Tune" on recorders (see figure 2.10). Add an accompaniment, or ask a student to add an accompaniment on the autoharp. Observe the arpeggiated melody and the fundamental chord structure.
5. Choose one or several students to perform the waltz steps while others play the "Swedish Tune."
6. Show the film "Vasen Street Live at StringNation 2007" featuring a trio of players—guitar, fiddle, and nyckle-harpa (a bowed lute with strings and keys, and sympathetic vibrating strings that sound when particular pitches are bowed). Draw attention to the interaction of three players, the shared melody, and the accented and unaccented pulses that are communicated without the need for a percussion instrument.
7. Locate Sweden on a map of Europe. Note the countries that surround Sweden and name the Scandinavian countries. Locate Germany (to the south), where the language and culture, including the music components of melody and rhythm, bear a resemblance to expressions of Swedish culture.

**Assessment**

1. Perform the melody on various classroom instruments.
2. Dance the waltz steps in a group, in a circle, line, or with partners.

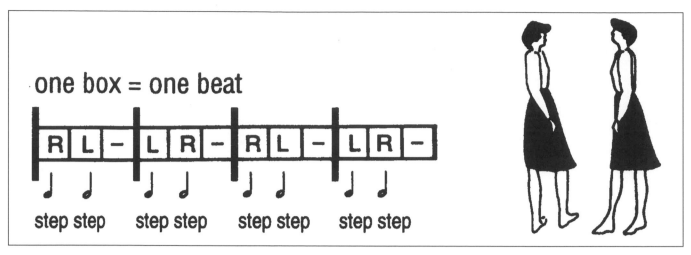

**Figure 2.5    Couples position, stepping in place**

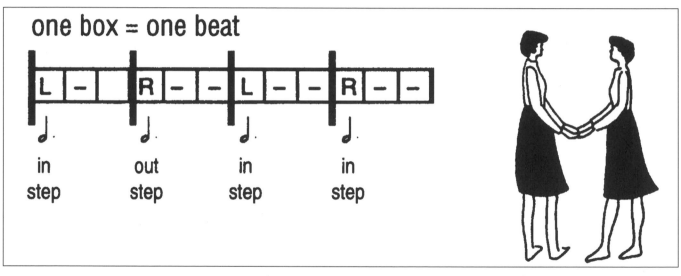

**Figure 2.6    Couples hold hands**

**Figure 2.7    Shoulder hold**

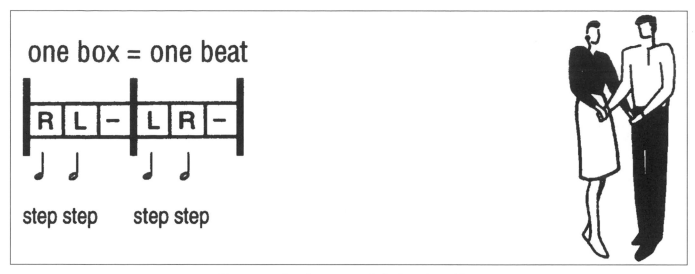

Figure 2.8   Couples promenade in skater's position

Figure 2.9   Inner and outer circles

**Figure 2.10**  "Swedish Tune"

# LESSON 3

## National Standards

- Singing, alone and with others, a varied repertoire of music
- Performing on instruments, alone and with others, a varied repertoire of music
- Listening to, analyzing, and describing music

## Objectives

Students will:

1. listen to songs that feature the yodel;
2. identify instruments of Austria and the alpine countries;
3. sing an Austrian folk song;
4. accompany the folk song with guitar or autoharp;
5. locate Austria, Bavarian Germany, and Switzerland on a map of Europe.

## Materials

1. Recording: "Ohne Text," featuring the Groupe Tirol (available from iTunes)
2. "Taylor Ware Yodeling" (available on www.youtube.com)
3. Guitar
4. Autoharp
5. Map of Europe

## Procedures

1. Play the recording, "Ohne Text" featuring the Groupe Tirol as an example of jodeler (jodel songs). Call attention to the preponderance of triple meter and to the arpeggiated melodies in major keys. Many yodel songs are organized into a verse-refrain form, the refrain of which is usually the yodeling of syllables rather than words.
2. Sing "The Cuckoo's Song" in unison, adding the harmony if appropriate for the age level (see figure 2.11). The language is an alpine Austrian dialect of German.

   *Pronunciation*

   Vehn dehr goo-goo-shrite, ahft ees lahng-ees-tsite.
   Veerd dehr schnee fehr-gehn, veern dee vees-lahn green.

3. While singing, add a pat-clap-snap gesture to keep the triple meter feeling.
4. Accompany the song on guitar or autoharp.
5. Show "Taylor Ware Yodeling," which features an eleven-year-old American girl who learned to yodel by listening to yodeling recordings.
6. On a map of Europe, locate the Germanic countries of Austria, Switzerland, and the southern part of Germany known as Bavaria. Discuss the possible reasons for the development of the yodel. Could it be that the Alps motivated people to sing from one mountain to the next for the pure enjoyment of the echo (in which case words were not necessary and the pitched cries of the arpeggiated melody collided into chords as they were bounced back to the singer)?

**Figure 2.11** "The Cuckoo's Song"

## Assessment

1. Perform "The Cuckoo's Song," singing and playing it on guitar or autoharp.
2. Describe a yodel.

## LESSON 4

**National Standard**

- Listening to, analyzing, and describing music

**Objectives**

Students will:

1. dance the branle, a French folk dance;
2. recognize the division of dance music into musical themes and phrases;
3. identify the sound of the concertina;
4. locate France on a map of Europe.

**Materials**

1. Recording: "Branle" from *The Dances of the World's Peoples*, vol. 2, *European Folk Dances*, Folkways Recordings (available from iTunes)
2. "Renaissance Dance" (available on www.youtube.com)
3. Map of Europe

**Procedures**

1. Play the recording of the branle, an old circle dance. The concertina (a small accordion) plays the melody and a second, larger accordion plays the accompaniment. Keep the steady beat by patting or clapping softly with two fingers.
2. Teach students to dance the branle. The formation is a circle, with hands joined (as shown in figure 2.12).

**Figure 2.12   Branle formation**

In the introduction, students bend their knees and bounce in place for sixteen beats. Follow these patterns for the dance, and repeat until the music's end:

*Part 1*

Move in the circle—eight running steps to the right and then eight running steps to the left—for sixteen beats.

*Part 2*

Standing in place, step and kick for sixteen beats, as shown in figure 2.13.

*Part 3*

Step and kick, moving into the circle for eight beats and out of the circle for eight beats, as shown in figure 2.14.

**Figure 2.13   Procedures for part 2**

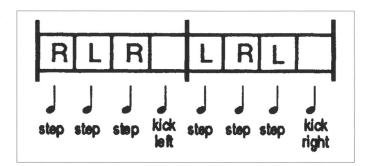

**Figure 2.14   Procedures for part 3**

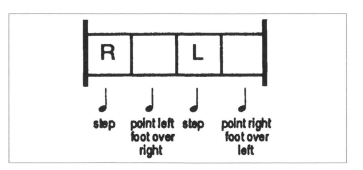

**Figure 2.15   Procedures for part 4**

*Part 4*

Each dancer stands in place and alternately points the left foot over the right foot and the right foot over the left foot, as shown in figure 2.15.

Repeat these steps as the dance music continues.

3.  Share a sampling of Renaissance dances that feature a consort of recorders, singers, keyboard and strings, and tambourine, on "Renaissance Dance," including the branle and other contemporary dance forms.
4.  Locate France on the map of Europe. Cousins of the branle are found throughout France and in many parts of Europe. Along the Pyrenees in the south, the Basques dance a similar circle dance called the sardana, and throughout most of Europe, people enjoy the communal spirit of dancing in a circle.

**Assessment**

1.  Dance a branle.

## LESSON 5

### National Standards

- Listening to, analyzing, and describing music
- Singing, alone and with others, a varied repertoire of music
- Performing on instruments, alone and with others, a varied repertoire of music
- Understanding music in relation to history and culture.

### Objectives

Students will:

1. listen to examples of Spanish dance songs;
2. recognize the importance and extent of dance music in Spain, including the fandango, seguidilla, and flamenco;
3. play the Andalusian cadence on the guitar;
4. play rhythmic ostinatos on the castanets;
5. play "Sequidillas de Castilla" as a video-demonstration of flamenco in action (available on www.youtube.com);
6. sing "Tío Pep;"
7. locate Spain on a map of Europe.

### Materials

1. Guitar
2. Castanets
3. Recording: "Three Flamenco Rhythms" (available from iTunes)
4. Map of Europe

### Procedures

1. Listen to "Three Flamenco Rhythms," which features guitar, castanets, and voice. Then listen again for the interplay of guitar and voice in the seguidilla, a flamenco-style dance song. Note the importance of the guitar's descending chord progression. Call attention to the melismatic melody of the seguidilla and to the shouts of joy and excitement.
2. Play the A minor, G major, F major, and E major chords in succession. This chord combination is known as the Andalusian cadence and is found in the music of southern Spain. Sing the root note as the cadence is played: A, G, F, and E. Listen again to "Three Flamenco Rhythms" for the cadence (see figure 2.16).

**Figure 2.16   Andalusian cadence**

**Figure 2.17　Spanish rhythms**

**Figure 2.18　"Tío Pep"**

3. Listen for the castanets again on "Three Flamenco Rhythms." Ask several students to play the Andalusian cadence on guitars, while others first clap and later play castanets for the Spanish rhythms shown in figure 2.17.
4. View the flamenco example "Seguidillas de Castilla." Challenge students to keep the pulse while they watch and listen to this spirited music.
5. Sing "Tío Pep," a folk song from central Spain (where the Andalusian sound is absent) (see figure 2.18). Note the use of melisma in the refrain (on the vocable "ah"). If guitar accompaniment is added, transpose to the key of D major. The text pronunciation is as follows:

> Lo tee-oh Pehp sehn vah Moo-roh, Tee-oh Pehp
> Day Moo-roh kaym pore-tah-rah, Tee-oh Pehp, Tee-oh Pehp.
> Oo-na tahr-tah-nah ee oon boo-roh Tee-oh Pehp
> Payr-nahr-sayn ah pahs-say-chahr Tee-oh Pehp, Tee-oh Pehp.

Translation:

> Old Uncle Joe's going to Muro, Uncle Joe.
> What will he bring back from town? Uncle Joe, Uncle Joe.

A two-wheeled cart and a burro, Uncle Joe.
So he can ride up and down, Uncle Joe, Uncle Joe.

6. Locate Spain on the map of Europe. Discuss the historical significance of Spain's proximity to North Africa, which is across the narrow Strait of Gibraltar. A report on the Moorish occupation of Spain over a seven-hundred-year period can help students place the country and its culture in perspective. The North African/Middle Eastern influence on the music is found in the melismatic singing, the somewhat free and flexible rhythm, and the evolution of the guitar from its predecessor, the Egyptian 'ud.

## Assessment

1. Sing the song, "Tío Pep," in tune and in time.
2. Play the Andalusian cadence on guitar.

## LESSON 6

### National Standards

- Singing, alone and with others, a varied repertoire of music
- Performing on instruments, alone and with others, a varied repertoire of music
- Listening to, analyzing, and describing music

### Objectives

Students will:

1. listen to "Trugnal mi Yane Sandanski, lele," a Bulgarian work song in 7/8 meter;
2. sing a Bulgarian song in 7/8 with drone;
3. play a Bulgarian song on recorders;
4. perform a Bulgarian dance;
5. identify the sound of the gaida bagpipes;
6. locate Bulgaria and Macedonia on a map of Europe.

### Materials

1. Recording: "Trugnal mi Yane Sandanski, lele," from *A Harvest, A Shepherd, A Mountain* (available on iTunes)
2. "The Mystery of Bulgarian Voices" (available on www.youtube.com)
3. Recorders
4. Map of Europe

### Procedures

1. Listen to "Trugnal mi Yane Sandanski, lele" (see figure 2.19) and tap the pulse of the 7/8 meter. Listen for the sound of the gaida bagpipes, the flute, and the various fiddles and lutes.

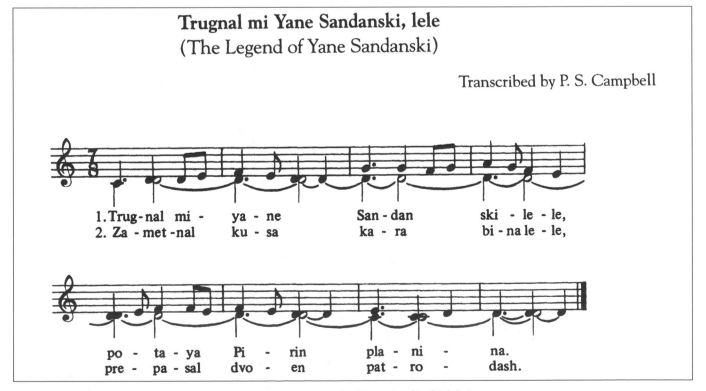

Figure 2.19 "Trugnal mi Yane Sandanski, lele"

**Figure 2.20**    "Trgnala mi Rumjana," collected by P. S. Campbell

2. The teacher should give the translation for the song: "Yane Sandanski sets off walking about the Pirin Mountains. He has a carbine over his shoulder; he has a double cartridge-belt. Yonder comes a young shepherd. Yane asks him: 'Didn't you see my people from my fighting band?' The young shepherd replies: 'Oh, Yane, up in the mountain, at the high peak of the Pirin Mountains you will find them.'" Explain that Yane was fighting the Turks, who occupied Bulgaria and most of the Balkans for about five hundred years.

3. Sing "Trugnal mi Yane Sandanski, lele," first in unison and later with the addition of the drone accompaniment. Note the only change that occurs: in measure seven, there is a shift from D to C and back to D again at measure eight. The text pronunciation is as follows:

> Troog-nahl mee Yah-neh Sahn-dahn-skee lay-lay
> Poh-tah-yah Pee-reen plah-nee-nah
> Zah-meht-nahl koo-sah kah-rah-bee-nah lay-lay
> Pray-pah-sahl dvoy-ehn pah-trohn-dahsh.

4. Play the Bulgarian dance song "Trgnala mi Rumjana" on recorders (see figure 2.20). The teacher should point out that the drone of the previous song and the harmony in thirds found in this song are characteristic of different regions of Bulgaria. Add to the recorders a chordal accompaniment on guitar or piano and a rhythmic pattern on a hand drum, as illustrated in figure 2.21.

5. Learn the following dance to accompany either 7/8 song: Have the students form a line with arms in a "W" (holding hands with arms crooked at elbow). Each dancer then steps to the right with the right foot and places the left foot behind the right. Students step right again and then place the left foot in front of the right. For the third measure, they step right and then left, bringing the feet together; and in the fourth measure of the dance

**Figure 2.21   Rhythm pattern on hand drum**

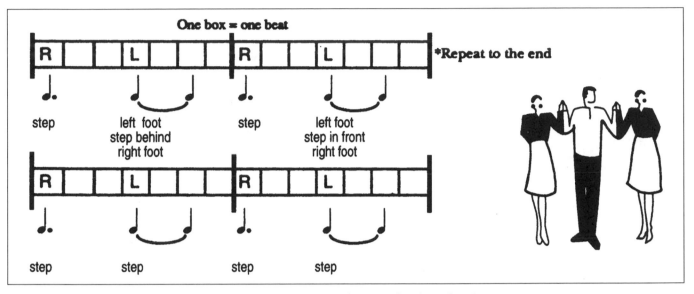

**Figure 2.22   Dance steps for "Trgnala mi Rumjana"**

pattern, step left and then right, bringing the feet together again. This pattern is repeated to the end of the music (see figure 2.22 for a diagram of the dance steps).

6. Locate Bulgaria on the map of Europe. Discuss the isolation of the Balkan countries from the European mainstream and their close proximity to Turkey and Asia Minor.

7. Share footage of "The Mystery of Bulgarian Voices" as exemplar of the choral music of Bulgaria, www.youtube.com, in which the singers feature the sounds of the drum strokes "dum" and "taka" in their first song. A second song, "Teodora," is one of the most widely known Bulgarian songs, the sung story of a maiden sleeping and dreaming of her loved one.

## Assessment

1. Perform the song "Trugnal mi Yane Sandanski, lele" vocally, on recorders, and as a dance.

## LESSON 7

### National Standards

- Singing, alone and with others, a varied repertoire of music
- Listening to, analyzing, and describing music

### Objectives

Students will:

1. sing a Hungarian folk song;
2. identify aspects of melody and rhythm that are typical of Hungarian folk music;
3. dance the csardas national dance;
4. listen to Kodály's Hungarian Rondo;
5. locate Hungary on a map of Europe.

### Materials

1. Recording: Zoltán Kodály, *Hungarian Rondo* (available on iTunes)
2. Map of Europe

### Procedures

1. Sing the song "The Forest" (see figure 2.23). Note the way in which the melody seems to focus on C, the fifth of the key, especially at the beginnings and endings of phrases one, two, and four. Note also the dotted rhythms, especially in measures three, seven, and fifteen. These are characteristic sounds of Hungarian folk music.
2. Dance the national folk dance of Hungary, the csardas. Students form a circle, either holding hands or with arms resting on neighbors' shoulders, and step, slide, and stomp, alternating motion to the right with motion to the left (see figure 2.24).
3. Through the efforts of Zoltán Kodály and Béla Bartók, Hungarian peasant music was collected and became the inspiration for many of their compositions. Kodály's *Hungarian Rondo* features "The Forest" as the A theme and four other folk songs in the contrasting sections. You can guide students in their listening by calling their attention to these items:

   *A theme*—"The Forest" theme played in a straightforward manner by strings, especially violins
   *B theme*—second folk song, played in conversation by clarinet and violins; stretched rubato tempo
   *A theme*—"The Forest" theme, third and fourth phrases only, played by violins
   *C theme*—third folk song, csardas-style accompaniment with cellos representing the "oom-pah-pah" of the cimbalom; virtuosic, gypsy-sounding violin melody
   *A theme*—"The Forest" for violin solo, partly minor harmony, fragments of melody, and slowing rubato tempo
   *D theme*—fourth folk song, strings sounding a syncopated accompaniment on the offbeats
   *E theme*—fifth folk song starting with bassoon and double bass; increased tempo with clarinet and then high strings on melody; drone-like reference to tonic
   *A theme*—"The Forest" theme, beginning with pulsing double bass drone; modulation of the theme and stretching of theme with slow tempo
   *E theme*—return to the fifth folk song; a festive dance ending

4. Locate Hungary on a map of Europe. Discuss the early origins of the people deep within the Russian interior and their migration westward to Hungary. Consider other events of a historical nature such as the Austro-Hungarian Empire and the Hungarian Revolution of 1956.

### Assessment

1. Sing the song, "The Forest."
2. Dance the czardas.

# The Forest

Figure 2.23 "The Forest"

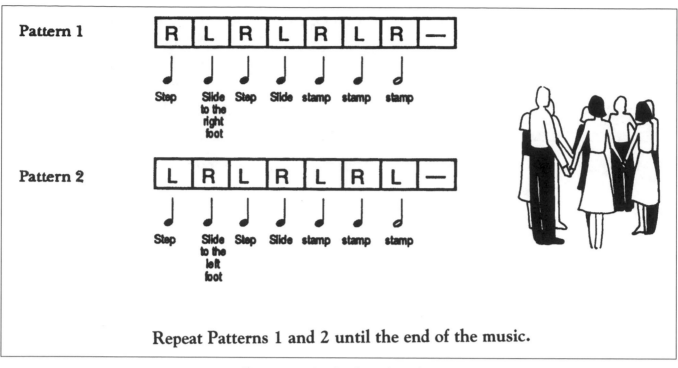

**Pattern 1**

R L R L R L R —

Step  Slide to the right foot  Step  Slide  stamp  stamp  stamp

**Pattern 2**

L R L R L R L —

Step  Slide to the left foot  Step  Slide  stamp  stamp  stamp

**Repeat Patterns 1 and 2 until the end of the music.**

**Figure 2.24  Csardas dance formation**

## NOTE

1. Download a map of Europe from *National Geographic* (www.nationalgeographic.com/xpeditions/atlas/), and project it on a screen for the students.

## DISCOGRAPHY

Altan. *Another Sky*. Virgin Records, 2000. Contemporary Irish traditional music from a leading band.

*Authentic Folk Music and Dances of the World*. Murray Hill S-4195 ("Seguidillas Guitano").

*Bavarian Yodeling Songs and Polkas*. Olympic 6115C. This recording includes songs and instrumental music with emphasis on the jodler, clog dancing, and polkas.

*The Chieftains 8*. Columbia 35726. A collection of Irish instrumental music, featuring the uilleann bagpipe, tin whistle, fiddle, harp, concertina, and the bodhran drum. The recording includes descriptive liner notes.

*Dances of the World's Peoples*. Vol. 2, *European Folk Dances*. Folkways FD 6502. Dance music for the Italian tarantella, French branle, Greek horo, Irish reel, and assorted Bulgarian dances. A pamphlet for learning the dance steps is included.

*Folk Fiddling from Sweden*. Nonesuch H-72033. Fiddle tunes from rural Sweden are performed on two fiddles, including dance music for vals, polska, and langdans.

*Folk Music from Norway*. Heilo NCD7078. Fiddle tunes and dance music for string and accordion ensembles.

*Greece Is . . . Popular and Folk Dances*. EMI 14C 062-70007. Contact Rashid Sales Company, 191 Atlantic Avenue, Brooklyn, NY 11201. Twelve Greek dances performed on bouzouki, santouri, and baglamas are presented, along with an instructional pamphlet.

*Hungarian Instrumental Music*. Hungariton LPX 18045-47. The most complete collection of Hungarian instrumental music, this four-record set contains examples of every Hungarian instrument, from the leaf to the cimbalom. A descriptive pamphlet accompanies the recordings.

*In Dublin's Fair City*. Olympic 6169. The Guinness Choir sings favorite Irish tunes.

*In the Shadow of the Mountain, Bulgarian Folk Music*. Nonesuch H-72038. Songs and instrumental music of southwestern Bulgaria (Pirin-Macedonian) are presented. The recording includes the diaphonic song style and the zurna, gaida, and gaydulka.

*Ivo Papazov and His Orchestra: Balkanology*. Nannibal HNCD1363. The virtuosity of Bulgarian wind-playing, featuring clarinet and saxophones, merges with jazz sensibilities and make for fiery music.

*Jodler und Schulplattler*. Fiesta FLPS 1905. Yodeling songs and folk dances that feature the boot slapping of men.

Kodály, Zoltán. *Hungarian Rondo*. Columbia MS 7034.

*Le Mystère des Voix Bulgares*. Explorer CD 79165-2. Women's choral songs, including dance melodies in 7/8 and 10/8.

Maccoll, Ewan, and Peggy Seeger. *The Long Harvest*, records 1 and 2. Argo ZDA 67. Write to 115 Fulham Road, London SW3. Traditional children's ballads are presented in English, Scottish, and North American variants, including "The Elfin Knight," "The Daemon Lover," and "Riddles Wisely Expounded." A pamphlet gives the text and origin of songs.

*Music and Song of Italy*. Tradition 1030. Everest Records, 10920 Wilshire Boulevard, Los Angeles, CA 90024. This recording includes songs and instrumental music from various regions of Italy, with liner notes that describe the influences of Albania, the Moors, and the Germanic countries. The performance of an ancient polyphonic song of Sardinia is a jewel in itself.

*Spain, World Library of Folk and Primitive Music*. Columbia 91A-02001. This recording includes music from all regions of Spain, including Andalusia, the Pyrenees, Galicia, and the Mediterranean. The attached booklet provides a background for each recorded selection.

*Spanish Folk Music*. Columbia World Library of Folk and Primitive Music, Spain, 91A-02001 ("Fandango de Comares").

*Swiss Yodeling Songs*. Olympic 6171. Ten Swiss yodelers perform these traditional songs.

## FILMOGRAPHY

*Le mystère des voix bulgares: A Bird Is Singing*. Produced in Berlin by Studio K7, documentation of a tour by the choral group.

*Riverdance—the Show*. Columbia/Tristar Studios, 1995. A brilliant pageant of traditional-yet-arranged Irish traditional music and dance, with a threading of romantic subplots that feature dancers Michael Flatley and Jean Butler.

## BIBLIOGRAPHY

Bartók, Béla, and Albert Lord. *Serbo-Croatian Folk Songs*. New York: Columbia University Press, 1951. The classic technical study of South Slavic traditional songs collected by Slavist Millman Parry. Transcriptions and texts of 205 women's songs with analysis.

Breathnach, Breandan. *Folk Music and Dances of Ireland*. Dublin: The Mercier Press, 1977. A comprehensive review of music and dance forms by a first-rate and highly regarded music scholar.

Bronson, Bertrand Harris. *The Traditional Tunes of the Child Ballads*. Vols. 1–4. Princeton, N.J.: Princeton University Press, 1959. The musical counterpart to the Francis James Child collection of English and Scottish ballads from the thirteenth to the nineteenth centuries. Tunes and texts are arranged by period for the study of ballads in England, Scotland, Ireland, and America.

Hast, Dorothea, and Stanley Scott. *Music in Ireland*. New York: Oxford University Press, 2004. An introduction to Irish traditional singing, instrumental music, and dance that reflect social values and political messages central to Irish identity, with ample exemplary selections on accompanying CD.

Karpeles, Maud. *Folk Songs of Europe*. London: Novello, 1956. A classic collection of texts and notations for European folk songs, transcribed by the author.

Kodály, Zoltán. *Folk Music of Hungary*. London: Barrie and Jenkins, 1971. Collected by Kodály, these songs represent the oral traditions of the Hungarian people. Several black-and-white photographs and illustrations of instruments are provided.

Lawson, Joan. *European Folk Dance*. London: Pitman Publishing, 1972. A description of folk dances from all of Europe, with instructions on specific movements. Melodies of dance songs are provided. The text also includes chapters on the development of the dances and costumes.

Lord, Albert. *The Singer of Tales*. Cambridge, Mass.: Harvard University Press, 1960. The author summarizes years of fieldwork among the Yugoslav epic singers and discusses the nature of the oral tradition; this is a revered historic text.

Nettl, Bruno. *Folk and Traditional Music of the Western Continents*. 3rd ed. Englewood Cliffs, N.J.: Prentice-Hall, 1990. This publication, which is an update of the 1973 version, is one of the most concise descriptions of European traditional music available. The author presents his thoughts on the character of European folk music and regional musics.

O'Canainn, Tomas. *Traditional Music in Ireland*. London: Routledge and Kegan Paul, 1978. The structure of traditional vocal and instrumental music is described, along with organological analysis of the uilleann pipes and fiddle. Excellent analysis of Sean-nos singing.

Rice, Timothy. *May It Fill Your Soul*. Chicago: University of Chicago Press, 1994. This is a description of music and music making in Bulgaria, including social and cognitive processes of music learning. Black-and-white photos, musical transcriptions, and a compact disc enhance descriptions.

———. *Music in Bulgaria*. New York: Oxford University Press, 2004. A concise introduction to the music of Bulgaria, with CD, and with consideration of its history and development in a nation undergoing change from agrarian to communist to postcommunist contemporary society.

# 3

# Euro-American Music

*Patricia Shehan Campbell and Ellen McCullough-Brabson*

There is a rich and colorful potpourri of American music that emanates from European expressions.[1] This is no wonder, since three-quarters of Americans can trace their lineage to Europe, so that the influences of "the Old World" of Europe appear at least marginally in their musical expressions. Think ballads, bluegrass, shape-note songs, polkas, and "Cajun"—for starters, and know that the essence of some Euro-American expressions is deeply embedded within America's musical soul.

"Euro-American" refers to the realm of Americans whose heritage is European, due to their birth in a European nation or through a lineage of ancestors who once lived there. People with Euro-American ancestry include Anglo-Americans, Irish Americans, German Americans, Italian Americans, Polish Americans, and Greek Americans, to name a few. If not themselves, then their parents, grandparents, or other family elders from earlier generations arrived in America from London or Limerick, Berlin or Bologna, Krakow or the island of Crete. Euro-American people often prefer to call themselves "American," disregarding the hyphenated identification altogether. When they can speak an American dialect of the English language, live within the laws of an American society, celebrate American national holidays, and deeply feel the spirit of an American democracy, then Euro-Americans are indeed American—regardless of their roots. They may have distinctive preferences in cuisine, routines and rituals, folklore and music that identify them with a European nation or culture, but these are blended, balanced, and colored by their time in living the American way.

Historically, the American "nation of immigrants" was a magnet for Europeans from every country on that continent. By 1750, the population of American citizens was decidedly tilted toward those of English ancestry, stemming from the shiploads of British colonists who had arrived to forge the American republic. These Anglo-Americans settled the coastal areas, from Boston north through Maine, down through New York and New Jersey, and all the way south from Virginia through the Carolinas. They were the hard-scrabble people who sought freedom from religious oppression, and were enticed by the promise of freedom to make their way forward in a rich and fertile land. More than any other group of people, the early Anglo-Americans were on the ground floor in revolutionizing and laying the foundation for a democratically governed republic.

Many Anglo-Americans soon moved inward to establish settlements along the eastern rivers, and into the Appalachian Mountains, where they staked out land in the hills and "hollers" of West Virginia, Kentucky, Tennessee, and elsewhere. They became known as "Appalachians," pronouncing the third syllable with a short "a" (as in "add") rather than with the long "a" of the academically preferred pronunciation. As they established their homes, they began to mix with the Cherokee and other native groups, and eventually with the Scots-Irish, Welsh, French, and African Americans. They worked hard on farms, in fields, and in the towns they were establishing, yet they also made some time for singing ballads, gathering for social dances, and making their weekly worship visits while singing church songs and hymns. When instruments became available to them, Anglo-Americans of the Southern Appalachian Mountains played their fiddles, dulcimers, banjos, and guitars on back porches, in barns, and in town halls. Regrettably, their rich culture came to be stereotyped as "hillbilly" in reference to the location of their homes in the beautiful Appalachian terrain known for bluegrass and country music, coal mining, and (in some sections) acute poverty. Yet they made their expressive marks early on in American culture, marks that continue on to this day.

The surge of Anglo-Americans was later joined by the Germans, followed by the nineteenth-century wave of Irish Catholics, and by the dawn of the twentieth century, Italians, various Slavic groups, and Greeks were arriving in droves in the United States. New mother-tongues were added to the streets of American neighborhoods, and new traditions—rituals, customs, and cuisines—joined cultural landscapes that had been principally Anglo-American in practice. An open-door policy brought Europeans of every size and shape to the shores of America—so much so that the Emergency Quota Act of 1921was enacted to cap immigration from Europe and elsewhere. This law succeeded in pulling up the drawbridge to America even while the "tenants of the castle" were already teeming with the new Europeans who teetered between their old and new worlds. An early twentieth-century Americanization process sought to turn immigrants from (especially) Eastern Europe and the Mediterranean into imitation Anglo-Saxons, even as the controversial concept of the melting-pot was countered by the more adventurous ideal of cosmopolitanism and America as "the first international nation." Yet while the various Euro-American groups blended somewhat into the mainstream cultural fabric of America, they often maintained their traditions.

Several Euro-American groups merit discussion here, in view of the music featured in this chapter: the Germanic and Slavic groups (such as the Bohemians, Germans, Poles, Slovenes, and Czechs) whose polka music is a notable addition to the American soundscape, and the Cajuns whose long-standing Louisiana communities shaped instrumental and vocal music that is as distinctive as their local dishes of gumbo, jambalaya, and crawfish etouffee.

The Germans contributed more immigrants in the American postcolonial period than any other country, including 15 percent of the total number of immigrants between 1820 and the mid-twentieth century. They settled especially in New York, Illinois, Ohio, Wisconsin, and Pennsylvania, and made their living early on in ways as diverse as craftsmen (bakers and carpenters), miners and mechanists, and professional teachers and physicians. The Czechs are the most western branch of the Slavs, coming from Bohemia and Moravia. They reached America in the late nineteenth century to farm on land that was then still cheap and plentiful. They established their schools, churches, and sokols (gymnastic societies) in Chicago, New York, and Cleveland, and in Midwestern states like Iowa and Wisconsin. Poles, or Polish Americans, are one of the largest ethnic groups in the United States, exiting Poland from the 1830s onward in search of the model liberal society they perceived America to be. Some young men were escaping military conscription in Poland, while others were looking to improve their economic status. The Poles settled in urban areas of the Middle Atlantic and Midwestern states, and worked in the mills, refineries, foundries, and slaughterhouses of Chicago, Cleveland, Toledo, Milwaukee, Omaha, and St. Louis. A south Slavic group, the Slovenes (or Slovenians), emigrated from their homeland to Midwestern cities where they could find work in factories, mines, and the lumber industry. Like the other Euro-American groups mentioned here, they built their lives around parish churches and the neighborhoods of restaurants, taverns, and shops they established.

The American culture know as "Cajun" is a corruption of the word Acadian, which refers to the French Catholic Acadians who were expelled by the British from their farms in the maritime provinces of Canada, and who then traveled to northern Maine and Louisiana. Nearly one million living in Louisiana identify themselves as Cajuns. Their original exile and suffering were immortalized by Henry Wadsworth Longfellow in the well-known poem, "Evangeline" (1847). Until Interstate Route 10 was cut through the bayous of southern Louisiana in the 1960s, the rural Cajun people existed in isolation in nearly inaccessible communities, and shaped their domestic arts at home, including a highly seasoned cuisine and a musical culture that is clearly identifiable by the sounds of fiddles, accordions, and the bright metallic sound of a silvery triangle. Cajuns once spoke almost exclusively their own dialect of French, worshiped at their own local Roman Catholic churches, and went to the small-town markets to buy their crawfish, etouffee, and hot boudan sausage. Cajun culture is still alive and well in Louisiana, even as the culture's music and cuisine are spread worldwide.

## CHARACTERISTICS OF EURO-AMERICAN MUSIC

### Folk Songs: Accent on Anglo-America

Cecil Sharp, an English scholar and musician, discovered a reservoir of Anglo-American music when he visited the Southern Appalachian Mountains in 1916. He found that English folk songs and ballads were still sung by the mountain people—songs that had been abandoned two and three centuries earlier in England. With his assistant Maud Karpeles, Sharp collected 1,612 songs in forty-eight weeks of travel through the rugged mountain terrain. Many of the songs made their way into the two-volume set *English Folk Songs from the Southern Appalachians*, which was published by Sharp in 1932, and a considerable number of them have formed the basis for contemporary Anglo-American music such as country and bluegrass.

Many Anglo-American folk songs make use of the pentatonic (five-note) scale, for example, "What'll I Do with the Baby-O," "Skin and Bones," "Sourwood Mountain," and "The Mockingbird." Other melodies are modal, based in the Ionian ("white note" scale starting on C), Dorian (starting on D), Mixolydian (starting on G), and Aeolian (starting on A). Examples of modally based songs are "Go Tell Aunt Rhody" (Ionian), "Skin and Bones" (Dorian), "Old Joe Clarke" (Mixolydian), and "The Wraggle Taggle Gypsies" (Aeolian). Most folk songs are based on four-phrase melodic structures, feature duple and triple meter, and are sung unaccompanied or are harmonized by dulcimer (plucked/ mountain or hammered), guitar, or banjo.

## Appalachian Ballads

A ballad is a song that tells a story. Appalachian ballads were traditionally performed by a solo, unaccompanied voice. They functioned as a source of entertainment, or sometimes to illustrate and transmit the ideals of socially acceptable behavior, such that characters in the ballad who did not behave correctly were punished. They transmitted ideas across a wide variety of topics: romance, humor, tragedy, happiness, religion, the supernatural, heroes, and historical events. Some of the better-known ballads include "Barbry Allen" (or "Barbara Allen"), "Twa Sisters" (or "Two Sisters"), and "The Wraggle-Taggle Gypsies." Francis James Child, an American scholar, grouped British (many of which were also Anglo-American) ballads in a collection of 305 genuine songs known collectively as the "Child Ballads." Their melodies were pentatonic and diatonic, and quite frequently modal.

## Instrumental Music of the Appalachians

During the formation of the American colonies, and in the postrevolutionary era, too, ensembles were formed to play serenades and divertimenti of Mozart and Haydn, and natural horns, clarinets, oboes, and bassoons joined stringed instruments. The American brass band tradition first emerged in the nineteenth century. In the Appalachian region, where settlements of poor English, Irish, and Scots arose from 1775 to 1850, folk tunes and ballads were sung and also played on fiddles, dulcimers, banjos, and guitars. The short bow sawstroke technique, developed by Scottish fiddler Neil Gow in the 1740s, defined Appalachian fiddling, and was featured in the performance of European waltzes, square dances, and reels. Many of the old-time fiddle tunes of Appalachia would have been associated with specific texts, including "Old Joe Clarke," "Sourwood Mountain," and "Lil' Liza Jane." The mountain dulcimer of three or four strings was frequently played in the mountain communities as a solo instrument, or to accompany folk songs and ballads. A "noter" (a small dowel) is utilized to play a melody against the two or three drone-strings of the dulcimer, and it sounds a whistling tone as it slides from fret to fret without leaving the string. The banjo came into use by Anglo-Americans of the Southern Mountains when black slaves introduced it (as a development of the West African halam). The guitar swept through Appalachia, largely as a result of Sears Roebuck & Co.'s mail-order campaign in the early twentieth century, so that even people in the most isolated communities could receive the instrument and teach themselves to play it.

## Shape-Note Music

Shape-note singing was once considered the domain of the rural South, and is associated with traditional Anglo-American sacred and secular songs (even while African Americans have also been active participants). The style is meant as a pedagogical tool, first developed in the early eighteenth century, for teaching people how to sight-read music through geometrically shaped notes that go beyond the usual round noteheads. The first publication to use shape-notes was *The Easy Instructor*, published in Albany, New York, in 1798 by William Little and William Smith. Shape-note singing flourished during the late eighteenth to the mid-nineteenth century. The North began gradually to reject this sight-singing method as European music and its solmization tradition was introduced and embraced, but shape-note singing survived and was continued in the South, particularly in the rural areas until well into the twentieth century. Today, people gather regularly to sing shape-note music outside of church venues for the sheer pleasure it brings them to vocalize the many modal and nondiatonic melodies that are preserved in this notation.

The four shapes in shape-note singing consist of a triangle for *fa*, a circle for *sol*, a rectangle for *la*, and a diamond for *mi*, all of which comprise what some have called "buckwheat notation." The use of the four solmization syllables, *fa*, *sol*, *la*, and *mi*, alleviates the need for singers to worry about keys, lines, or spaces to read music. The shape-note system is based on a moveable *do*. No matter what key signature or clef sign is used, scale degrees have the same note syllables and the shapes and intervals between them remain constant. Accidentals are represented by the syllables *fi*, *si*, and *li* for sharps and *say*, *lay*, and *may* for flats. There is also a seven-shape notation that developed after the four-shape system, which uses a separate shape for each solmization syllable.

Shape-note music is sung a cappella and in three- or four-part harmony. Singers include trained and untrained voices, many who sing loudly at the top of their lungs. There are no auditions, rehearsals, or audiences in the style; everyone is welcome to sing. A hollow square is the traditional seating arrangement for shape-note choirs, where all rows face center. The tenors and altos face each other, the basses sit to the tenors' left and the treble singers sit to the tenors' right. The melodic tenor part is sung by men and women in octaves. One of the most popular shape-note books is *The Sacred Harp*, first published in 1844 and still used today, where over 600 plain tunes, fuguing tunes, anthems, and canons are gathered together.

## Bluegrass Music

Bluegrass is an Anglo-American "roots music," popular in the Appalachian and Ozark mountains, and stemming from the traditional music brought by the English, Irish, and Scottish settlers. It is traditionally played by acoustic stringed instruments such as guitar, the five-string banjo, fiddle (or mandolin), and upright, nonelectric bass. Bill Monroe is referred to as the founding father of bluegrass music, taking the name of the band he formed in 1939, the Blue Grass Boys. It is an amalgam of old-time music, country, ragtime, and jazz. It was first used for dancing in the rural areas, but eventually was spread to more urban areas. As in jazz, bluegrass players perform together and also take turns improvising the melody. Some of the great bluegrass players include the Stanley Brothers, Lester Flatt and Earl Scruggs with the Foggy Mountain Boys, and Jimmy Martin and the Osborne Brothers (in a first bluegrass generation), and Del McCoury, John Hartford, and Ricky Skaggs (and his "newgrass" music).

## Cajun Music of French Louisiana

The French Louisiana sound of Cajun music (and its Cajun-influenced and Creole-based zydeco form) is clearly identifiable by its accordion, fiddle, and triangle, driving pulse, and basic tonic and dominant harmonies. Much of the standard repertoire of Cajun music stems from the 1920s and 1930s, and included fiddle double stops, staccato-style notes, and major-keyed melodies. In the renaissance of Cajun music (about 1975), the double stops are missing, dominant blues chords are heard, and folk, jazz, and bluegrass elements are incorporated by players such as Michael Doucet and BeauSoleil. Yet even as Cajun music turned toward Texas Swing, or went "Dancehall," or moved in the direction of R & B, rock, and zydeco, the older traditions are preserved by the likes of Eddie LeJeune and Robert Jardell. Cajun music is alive and well at festivals and dance halls, and at weddings and reunions in Louisiana's Cajun country.

## Polkas of German and Slavic Americans

Originating in Central Europe, the polka is a fast and lively dance that is commonly heard at social celebrations of German and Slavic Americans. Polkas feature duple meter, accordions, bass, drums, and sometimes trumpets and tubas (and even banjos and violins!). There are several polka styles, including a Chicago style (with or without clarinet and trumpet), a Slovenian style (associated with Cleveland), and a "Dutchman style" with a tuba's *oom-pah* sound that is principally Germanic in flavor. There is even the "conjunto-style" polkeros, which reflects the merging of the music of the Germans and Wends with the Mexican American sensibilities. A number of organizations exist to preserve the cultural heritage of polka music, including the International Polka Association and the United States Polka Association.

# LESSON 1: AN APPALACHIAN SONG THAT TELLS A STORY

## National Standards

- Singing, alone and with others, a varied repertoire of music
- Listening to, analyzing, and describing music

## Objectives

Students will:

1. listen to and sing "Mister Frog Went A-Courtin'" and accompany the song on a dulcimer;
2. identify the characteristics of a ballad;
3. compare and contrast two recordings of "Mister Frog Went A-Courtin'";
4. watch several video versions of "Mister Frog Went A-Courtin'" (or "Froggie Went A-Courtin'");
5. locate the Southern Appalachian Mountains on the map of the United States.

## Materials

1. A map of the United States
2. Recordings:
   a. "Frog Went A-Courtin'," featuring George and Gerry Armstrong (available from www.folkways.si.edu)
3. Video recordings:
   a. "Froggie Went A-Courtin'," featuring Bruce Springsteen and friends (www.youtube.com)
4. Dulcimer or guitar
5. A picture book of the song/story, for example, "Froggie Went A-Courting" by Chris Conover (New York: Farrar, Strauss and Giraux, 1986)
6. Music notation for "Mister Frog Went A-Courtin'" (see figure 3.1)

## Procedures

1. Introduce a ballad as a song that tells a story. Describe the presence of ballads among Anglo-Americans living in the Appalachian Mountains. Locate this area on a map of the United States.
2. Sing the song "Mister Frog Went A-Courtin'."
3. Tell the history of the song. "Mister Frog Went A-Courtin'" is an Anglo-American children's song that has existed for more than four hundred years. There are more than 200 variations of the tune and text of this ballad, due to the fact that it was passed on from one generation to the next by oral tradition rather than by music notation. In some accounts of the story, the mouse lived happily ever after with the frog, rather than being swallowed. Curiously, when there were good times for the common people, the song had a happy ending, and when the times were bad, the ending was sad. Another variation of the song suggests that Miss Mouse represented Queen Elizabeth I of England and Mister Frog was the French ambassador to the English court, le Duc d'Alencon, who wanted to marry her. The song was used as a social protest against the marriage.
4. Use a storybook of the song/story to illustrate the lyrics.
5. Teach the song to students in the oral tradition, by singing it and having students join in as they can.
6. Play two recorded versions of the song for students to listen to. Challenge them to find similarities and differences between the renditions, as per the rhythm, lyrics, melody, and texture.
7. Play the melody on the dulcimer, strumming the drone strings along with the melody. As an alternative, provide a harmonic accompaniment on the guitar.
8. Watch a video recording of "Froggie Went A-Courtin'," featuring Bruce Springsteen and friends. Ask how this version is related to the version just learned.
9. As an extension, write new verses to the song, imaging new events that could happen in the lives of the frog and the mouse.

---

This lesson was prepared by Ellen McCullough-Brabson and Patricia Shehan Campbell.

### Mister Frog Went A-Courtin'

Appalachian Song

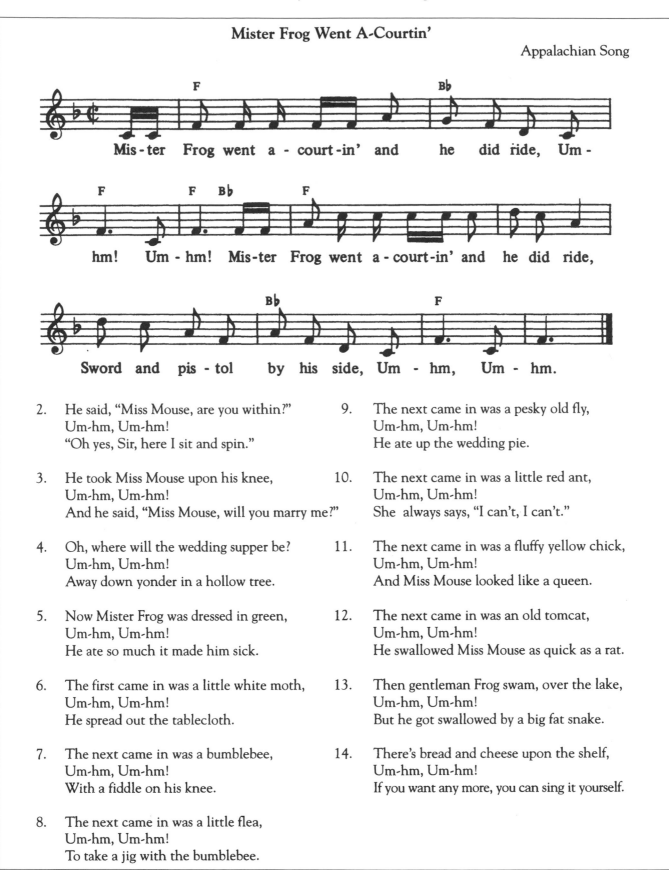

Mis-ter Frog went a-court-in' and he did ride, Um-
hm! Um-hm! Mis-ter Frog went a-court-in' and he did ride,
Sword and pis-tol by his side, Um-hm, Um-hm.

2. He said, "Miss Mouse, are you within?"
Um-hm, Um-hm!
"Oh yes, Sir, here I sit and spin."

3. He took Miss Mouse upon his knee,
Um-hm, Um-hm!
And he said, "Miss Mouse, will you marry me?"

4. Oh, where will the wedding supper be?
Um-hm, Um-hm!
Away down yonder in a hollow tree.

5. Now Mister Frog was dressed in green,
Um-hm, Um-hm!
He ate so much it made him sick.

6. The first came in was a little white moth,
Um-hm, Um-hm!
He spread out the tablecloth.

7. The next came in was a bumblebee,
Um-hm, Um-hm!
With a fiddle on his knee.

8. The next came in was a little flea,
Um-hm, Um-hm!
To take a jig with the bumblebee.

9. The next came in was a pesky old fly,
Um-hm, Um-hm!
He ate up the wedding pie.

10. The next came in was a little red ant,
Um-hm, Um-hm!
She always says, "I can't, I can't."

11. The next came in was a fluffy yellow chick,
Um-hm, Um-hm!
And Miss Mouse looked like a queen.

12. The next came in was an old tomcat,
Um-hm, Um-hm!
He swallowed Miss Mouse as quick as a rat.

13. Then gentleman Frog swam, over the lake,
Um-hm, Um-hm!
But he got swallowed by a big fat snake.

14. There's bread and cheese upon the shelf,
Um-hm, Um-hm!
If you want any more, you can sing it yourself.

**Figure 3.1** "Mister Frog Went A-Courtin'"

10. As demonstration of the process of the oral tradition, play the "gossip game," in which one person creates a simple story of about three sentences. For example, "There was a little girl and boy. They met a friendly fox in the forest, who taught them a fox dance. They shared the fox dance with all their friends." One person whispers the story to the next person, who whispers it to the next, and so on. This continues until everyone has heard the story. The last person speaks the story out loud. Probably, the last version will be quite different from the first. This activity will show how a folk song or ballad can also undergo radical changes as it is orally transmitted.

**Assessment**

1. Sing the song, with melody and lyrics intact.
2. Listen and describe similarities and differences between the two renditions of "Frog Went A-Courtin'."

## LESSON 2: A CHILD BALLAD

### National Standards

- Singing, alone and with others, a varied repertoire of music
- Listening to, analyzing, and describing music
- Performing on instruments, alone and with others, a varied repertoire of music

### Objectives

Students will:

1. listen to the story, "Sody Sallyraytus";
2. listen to and sing "Gypsy Davy" or "The Wraggle-Taggle Gypsies" and watch a puppet dramatization of the story;
3. discuss the important of oral tradition in Anglo-American music of the Southern Appalachians;
4. identify a child ballad.

### Materials

1. Finger puppets that represent one male and two female gypsies, the lady and lord of the manor, and a servant
2. "Sody Sallyraytus" in *Grandfather Tales* by Richard Chase (Boston: Houghton Mifflin, 1948)
3. Recordings:

    a. "Gypsy Laddie" ("Gypsy Davy") performed by Jean Ritchie (available from www.folkways.si.edu)
    b. "Gypsy Dave" ("Gypsy Davy") performed by Cisco Houston (available from www.folkways.si.edu)

4. Video: "The Wraggle-Taggle Gypsies," featuring Andreas Scholl (www.youtube.com)
5. Guitars or autoharps
6. Music notation for "The Wraggle-Taggle Gypsies" (see figure 3.2)

### Procedures

1. Tell the tale "Sody Sallyraytus," just to bring students into the realm of storytelling—a true performance art in the hands of Appalachian people.
2. Sing "The Wraggle-Taggle Gypsies," a variant of "Gypsy Davy." With young students, act out the story with finger puppets.
3. Teach the song "The Wraggle-Taggle Gypsies" to students. Observe the oral tradition, or use the notation provided.
4. Listen to two recordings of the song (also known as "Gypsy Davy," "Gypsy Laddie," and "Gypsy Dave"). Discuss the variations of tune and text, and note that this is a result of the oral tradition. Explain that the song is a Child ballad, noting the information provided at the chapter's beginning.
5. View the video of "The Wraggle-Taggle Gypsies," listening to the clear, high sound of the countertenor, Andreas Scholl. Ask students to comment on this version compared to the earlier recordings. Which version do they prefer? Why?
6. While singing, play a basic chordal accompaniment to "The Wraggle-Taggle Gypsies" on guitars and autoharps. Chording once per beat, or every two beats, is sufficient, while some may wish to embellish the pattern slightly, sounding a successive quarter- and two eighth-note pattern (see figure 3.3).
7. Listen to other examples of Child ballads as sung by Jean Ritchie and Cisco Houston, on the same recordings.
8. Read other stories from the Southern Appalachian Mountains, from the Gilbert Chase collection.
9. Have the students make their own finger puppets for "The Wraggle-Taggle Gypsies," so that they might enact the characters and events of the ballad.

This lesson was prepared by Ellen McCullough-Brabson and Patricia Shehan Campbell.

# The Wraggle-Taggle Gypsies

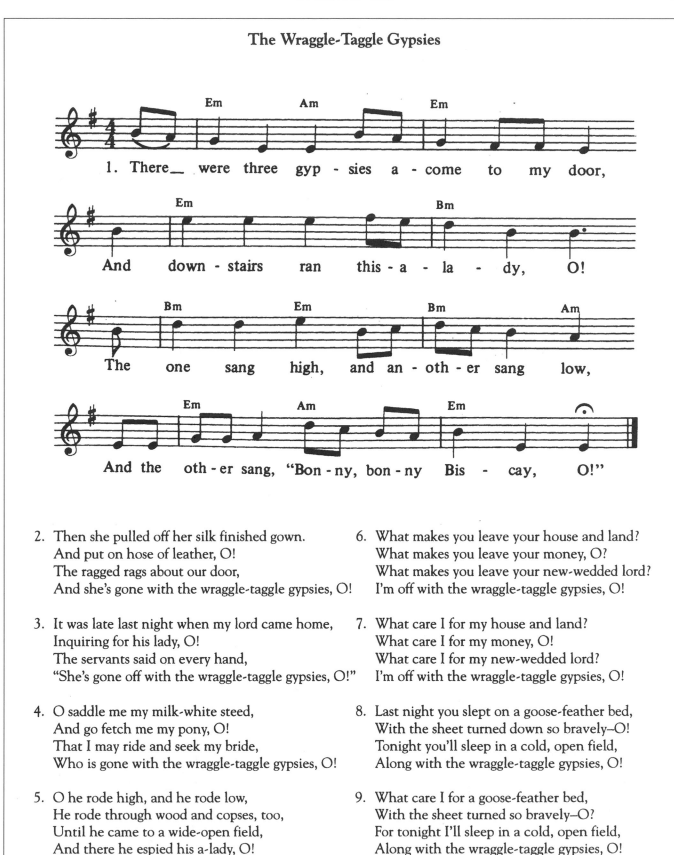

2. Then she pulled off her silk finished gown.
   And put on hose of leather, O!
   The ragged rags about our door,
   And she's gone with the wraggle-taggle gypsies, O!

3. It was late last night when my lord came home,
   Inquiring for his lady, O!
   The servants said on every hand,
   "She's gone off with the wraggle-taggle gypsies, O!"

4. O saddle me my milk-white steed,
   And go fetch me my pony, O!
   That I may ride and seek my bride,
   Who is gone with the wraggle-taggle gypsies, O!

5. O he rode high, and he rode low,
   He rode through wood and copses, too,
   Until he came to a wide-open field,
   And there he espied his a-lady, O!

6. What makes you leave your house and land?
   What makes you leave your money, O?
   What makes you leave your new-wedded lord?
   I'm off with the wraggle-taggle gypsies, O!

7. What care I for my house and land?
   What care I for my money, O!
   What care I for my new-wedded lord?
   I'm off with the wraggle-taggle gypsies, O!

8. Last night you slept on a goose-feather bed,
   With the sheet turned down so bravely–O!
   Tonight you'll sleep in a cold, open field,
   Along with the wraggle-taggle gypsies, O!

9. What care I for a goose-feather bed,
   With the sheet turned so bravely–O?
   For tonight I'll sleep in a cold, open field,
   Along with the wraggle-taggle gypsies, O!

**Figure 3.2** "The Wraggle-Taggle Gypsies"

**Figure 3.3   Chording rhythm for guitars or autoharps**

**Assessment**

1. Sing the ballad of "The Wraggle-Taggle Gypsies" from memory.
2. Play a basic chordal accompaniment to the ballad, while singing.
3. Describe the features of a ballad.

## LESSON 3: FROM FOLK SONG TO FIDDLE TUNE, "OLD JOE CLARKE"

### National Standards

- Singing, alone and with others, a varied repertoire of music.
- Listening to, analyzing, and describing music.
- Performing on instruments, alone and with others, a varied repertoire of music.

### Objectives

Students will:

1. listen to "Old Joe Clarke" and identify Mixolydian mode in the verse and chorus of the song;
2. sing "Old Joe Clarke" and create new verses;
3. listen to recordings of "Old Joe Clarke" that feature vocal and instrumental components.

### Materials

1. Recordings:
   a. "Old Joe Clark," featuring Paul Clayton (dulcimer/vocal) (available from www.folkways.si.edu)
   b. "Old Joe Clark," featuring Pete Seeger (banjo/vocal) (available from www.folkways.si.edu)
   c. "Old Joe Clark," featuring Tracy Schwarz (fiddle) (available from www.folkways.si.edu)
   d. "Old Joe Clark," featuring The Bluegrass Buddies (full bluegrass band) (available from www.folkways .si.edu)
2. Video: Various versions of "Old Joe Clarke" (www.youtube.com)
3. Available Appalachian folk instruments, such as dulcimer, banjo, fiddle, guitar, mandolin
4. Music notation for "Old Joe Clarke" (see figure 3.4)
5. Violins (fiddles) and dulcimers

### Procedures

1. Sing the song "Old Joe Clarke." As students become familiar with the chorus through repeated listenings, ask students to join in singing it.
2. Have the students listen to the four recordings of "Old Joe Clarke." Challenge them to identify the folk instruments they hear: dulcimer, banjo, fiddle, guitar, mandolin. Direct their attention to the melody, and ask them to discern any differences between the instrumental renditions of it.
3. Teach the students to sing "Old Joe Clarke." Note especially that they strive to sing accurately the lowered seventh degree as C natural (rather than C sharp).
4. Invite students to sing with the recordings. Discuss the various styles, and why some versions are easier than others to follow and sing with.
5. Invite a fiddler (or player of dulcimer, banjo, or mandolin) to visit and perform for the students. Have questions ready to set the conversation running for the students, such as "How did you learn to play?" "Do you learn by ear or by note (or both)?" "Why did you choose to play this instrument?" "Do you enjoy playing alone and/or together with other musicians?"
6. Invite students of violin to "figure out" the melody for "Old Joe Clarke" on their instruments. Bring one or more dulcimers into the classroom, and invite students to explore and experiment with play the melody they have sung on this Anglo-American instrument.
7. View a selection of video examples of "Old Joe Clarke," noting the variety of styles in which the song has been played and sung.

---

This lesson was prepared by Ellen McCullough-Brabson and Patricia Shehan Campbell.

## Old Joe Clarke

**Verses**

1. Old Joe Clarke he had a house, Fif-teen stor-ies high, And ev-'ry stor-y in that house Was filled with chick-en pie.

**Chorus**

Fare ye well, Old Joe Clarke, Fare ye well, I say. Fare ye well, Old Joe Clarke, I'm a-goin' a-way.

2. Old Joe Clarke he had a mule,
[It's name]* was Morgan Brown,
And ev'ry tooth in that mule's head
Was sixteen inches 'round.

3. Old Joe had a yellow cat,
[She'd nei]*ther sing nor pray,
(She) stuck her head [in the]* [butter]*milk jar
To work her sins a-way.

4. I went down to Old Joe's house,
[Never]* been there before,
(and) He slept on a feather bed
And I slept on the floor.

5. Sixteen horses in my team,
The leaders they are blind,
There's a pretty girl on my mind.
And every time the sun goes down

6. Eighteen miles of mountain road
And fifteen miles of sand,
If I ever travel this road again,
I'll be a married man.

*Sing the two syllables that are enclosed in brackets on one note.*

**Figure 3.4 "Old Joe Clarke"**

**Assessment**

1. Accurately sing "Old Joe Clarke," with all six verses of text.
2. Discriminate among the recorded renditions of "Old Joe Clarke," and discuss their similarities and differences.
3. Play "Old Joe Clarke" on fiddle or dulcimer.

## LESSON 4: SHAPE-NOTE SINGING

### National Standards

- Singing, alone and with others, a varied repertoire of music
- Reading and notating music
- Listening to, analyzing, and describing music

### Objectives

Students will:

1. listen to "Singing School," which features shape-note singers, and discuss the singing style;
2. listen to various other shape-note recordings, in order to instill the characteristic sound;
3. list characteristics of shape-note singing;
4. view the shape-note musical notation for "Happy Birthday, Anita" and practice chanting each part with the *sol–fa* syllables;
5. sing one or more lines of "Happy Birthday, Anita" with the traditional words;
6. watch the segment on shape-note singing featured in the DVD *Amazing Grace with Bill Moyers* and in the segment from *Cold Mountain*.

### Materials

1. "Happy Birthday, Anita" music in shape-note music notation
2. "Welcome, Welcome, Ev'ry Guest" music in shape-note music notation
3. Recordings:

    a. "Singing School," from *The Social Harp: Early American Shape-Note Songs*, led by Hugh McGraw (available on Rounder)
    b. "Old Harp Singing," featuring Old Harp Singers from Eastern Tennessee (available from www.folkways .si.edu)

5. Video:

    a. *Cold Mountain*, movie (2003)
    b. Church hymn, "I'm Going Home" (www.youtube.com)

4. *Amazing Grace with Bill Moyers*, DVD, Pacific Arts Video (1990)
5. Map of the United States

### Procedures

1. Play recordings of shape-note singing. Ask students to identify musical characteristic representative of this singing style. Prompt for these responses: the use of solfège fasola syllables, harmony, (often) modal melody, lack of instrumental accompaniment, (typical) sacred or church-related text, (often) loud dynamic level.
2. Show students shape-note music notation. Give a brief history of shape-note singing and explain how the system works (see figure 3.5). Arrange chairs in a traditional shape-note singing setup, a hollow-square with all four rows facing center.
3. Using the tenor line first, practice singing each part of "Happy Birthday, Anita" (see figure 3.6) with shape-notes. Combined several lines, or all lines. Once the shape-notes have been mastered, sing the song using the traditional words with two or more parts.
4. Watch the shape-note singing segment found in the DVD *Amazing Grace with Bill Moyers* and on the segment from *Cold Mountain*. Discuss the singing quality, the singers, the song leader, the setup of the room/space for the singers, and any other details that students may observe.
5. Take a familiar (and simple) melody and rewrite it using shape-notes. For example, "Amazing Grace," "Auld Lang Syne," or "America (My Country 'Tis of Thee)."

---

This lesson was prepared by Ellen McCullough-Brabson and Patricia Shehan Campbell.

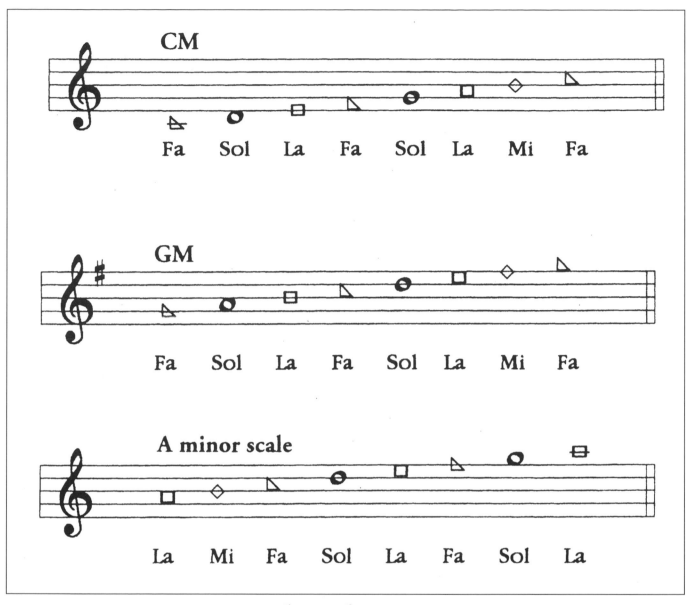

**Figure 3.5   Shape-notes**

6. On a map of the United States, locate the areas in which shape-note singing has been especially popular—first in the north (New York and into the New England states) and then across the south, from Mississippi, Alabama, and Georgia, into the Carolinas, and over to Missouri.

**Assessment**

1. Sing a shape-note song with correct melody and text.
2. Read with success a shape-note song, using the fasola solfège syllables.
3. Describe the qualities and characteristics of shape-note singing.

# Happy Birthday, Anita

Arranged by Hugh McGraw

**Figure 3.6** "Happy Birthday, Anita"

## LESSON 5: BLUEGRASS MUSIC

### National Standards

- Singing, alone and with others, a varied repertoire of music
- Listening to, analyzing, and describing music

### Objectives

Students will:

1. listen to recorded examples of bluegrass music, particularly the song "In the Pines";
2. sing a bluegrass song, "In the Pines";
3. play guitar chords for "In the Pines";
4. view films of bluegrass music, featuring "In the Pines" and "Rocky Top";
5. become familiar with other bluegrass tunes.

### Materials

1. Guitars
2. Video:

   a. "In the Pines," featuring Bill Monroe and the Bluegrass Boys (www.youtube.com/watch?v=ASZl4Z54Sbg)
   b. "Tennessee Rocky Top," video of bluegrass music/culture images (www.youtube.com/watch?v=c3Ku97TzeOg)
3. Recordings:

   a. "In the Pines," featuring Roscoe Holcomb on *The High Lonesome Sound* (available from www.folkways.si.edu)
   b. "In the Pines," featuring the Virginia Mountain Boys (available from www.folkways.si.edu)
4. Music notation for "In the Pines" (see *Tunes and Grooves*, p. 178)
5. Map of the United States

### Procedures

1. Have the students listen to recordings of "In the Pines," as performed by Roscoe Holcomb and the Virginia Mountain Boys.
2. Enumerate some of the stylistic features of bluegrass music: (typically) both instrumental and voices, use of acoustic instruments (featuring guitar, banjo, fiddle or mandolin, upright bass), (often) diatonic melodies of major quality, forms that feature full ensemble and sections for instrumental improvisatory solos.
3. Sing the song, "In the Pines," running through all twenty verses. Note that this version was first recorded by Bill Monroe and the Blue Grass Boys in 1941 for RCA Victor, and became one of their signature songs in the rise of the bluegrass movement in the 1940s and 1950s (see figure 3.7).
4. Play the chords as designed on guitar, plucking the bass or root note on beat 1 and strumming the chord on beats 2 and 3. The accompaniment pattern is as follows:

   | 3/4 | B/r | Ch | Ch |
   |-----|-----|----|----|
   |     | 1   | 2  | 3  |

   [B/r = bass/root note, plucked; Ch = chord strummed]

5. View the film *In the Pines* featuring Bill Monroe and the Blue Grass Boys. Note the interaction of the musicians, and the manner in which the instrumentalists come forward or are highlighted as they play solo.
6. View the film *Tennessee Rocky Top* to hear the well-known bluegrass song "Rocky Top," while also taking in images of bluegrass culture.

---

This lesson was prepared by Patricia Shehan Campbell.

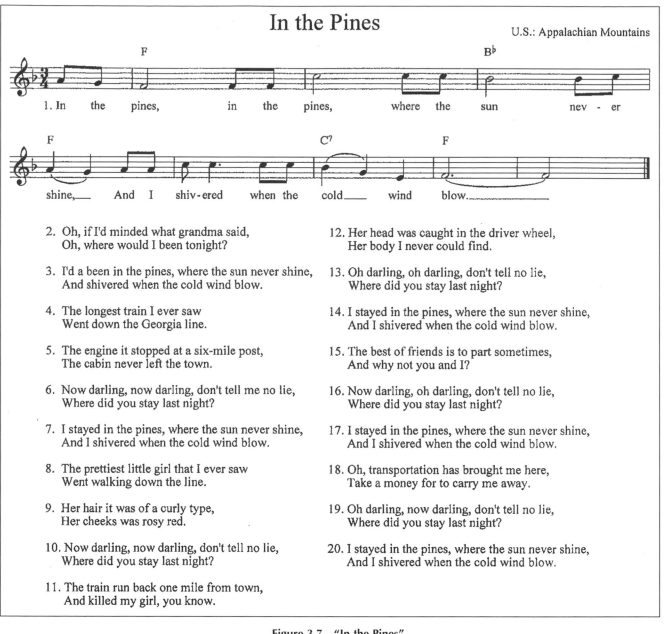

**Figure 3.7 "In the Pines"**

From *Tunes and Grooves for Music Education*, Pearson, © 2008. Used with permission.

7. As an extension, search the Internet for recordings and lyrics of other well-known bluegrass songs, including "Rocky Top," "Shady Grove," "Knoxville Girl," "Long Black Veil," "Cindy," "Blue-Eyed Gal," "Cripple Creek," "Wildwood Flower," and "John Henry." Learn to sing and play them.
8. Locate "bluegrass country" on a map of the United States, particularly Virginia, West Virginia, Kentucky, Tennessee, the southern hills of Ohio and Indiana, the northern reaches of Georgia and Alabama, and the western ends of North and South Carolina.

## Assessment

1. Sing "In the Pines" accurately, in tune, and in time.
2. Describe bluegrass music and its cultural context.

## LESSON 6: MUSIC FROM CAJUN COUNTRY

### National Standards

- Singing, alone and with others, a varied repertoire of music
- Listening to, analyzing, and describing music
- Playing on instruments, alone and with others, a varied repertoire of music

### Objectives

Students will:

1. listen to recordings of Cajun music;
2. sing a Cajun-style song, "Allons Danser, Colinda";
3. play guitar and triangle to "Allons Danser, Colinda";
4. view video recordings of Cajun musicians.

### Materials

1. Guitars
2. Triangles
3. Recordings:

   a. Michael Doucet and friends in "From Now On" (available from www.folkways.si.edu)
   b. Various artists in *Cajun Social Music* (available from www.folkways.si.edu)
   c. Roy Brule, in "Allons Danser, Colinda" (available from www.folkways.si.edu)

4. Video:

   a. Michael Doucet and BeauSoleil (www.youtube.com/watch?v=1lul1A2c73g)
   b. BeauSoleil (www.youtube.com/wagtch?v=mvXGJ8eP180)

5. Notation for "Allons Danser, Colinda" (see *Tunes and Grooves*, p. 19)
6. Map of the United States

### Procedures

1. Listen to examples of the award-winning Cajun fiddler Michael Doucet play traditional and contemporary tunes in Cajun style, on "From Now On." Sample "Le Two-Step de Basile," "L'amour ou la folie," "Madame Boudreaux," "Fonky Bayou," and "New Orleans." Note the florid nature of the fiddle's fast-moving, elaborated melody.
2. Listen to examples of a full Cajun band, in "Courtableau" and "Osson Two-Step" (from *Cajun Social Music*). Identify the sounds of the accordion, fiddle, guitar, and the triangle.
3. Learn the song "Allons Danser, Colinda" as an example of sung Cajun music, in order to reinforce that this genre extends across instrumental and vocal styles (see figure 3.8).
4. Play the chords to the melody on guitar, strumming up and down in eighth-note strums to this pattern, accenting the first beat.
5. Play the Cajun-style "chinky-chink" rhythm on a triangle (see figure 3.9).
6. Listen to the recording of "Allons Danser, Colinda" by Roy Brule. Try dancing a two-step, with partners circling round across the floor in a lightly bouncing step-step-step-pause movement.
7. Find the state of Louisiana on a map of the United States, and note especially the region west of New Orleans, south of Baton Rouge, and the city of Lafayette that is regarded as the center of Cajun country.

---

This lesson was prepared by Patricia Shehan Campbell.

**Figure 3.8   "Allons Danser, Colinda"**

2. C'est pas tout le monde quit connait,
Danser les danses du vieux temps.
Allons, danser, Colinda
Pour faire fâcher les vieilles femmes.

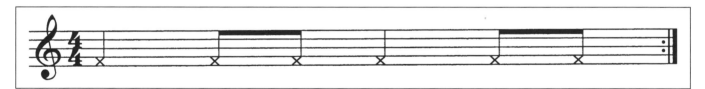

**Figure 3.9   Cajun-style chinky-chink rhythm**

### Assessment

1. Sing a Cajun song, "Allons Danser, Colinda," with accuracy of melody and rhythm.
2. Describe Cajun music.
3. Play an accompaniment to a Cajun song.

## LESSON 7: POLKA TIME!

### National Standards

- Listening to, analyzing, and describing music
- Singing, alone and with others, a varied repertoire of music

### Objectives

Students will:

1. locate polka territories (cultures) on maps of Europe and the United States;
2. listen to a variety of polka bands from the American Midwest, directing their attention to instruments, rhythms, meters, and tempi of the dance music;
3. observe polka musicians and dancers on video clips;
4. sing or hum the melodies of various polka tunes;
5. interact with a polka musician and/or dancer in residence.

### Materials

1. Recordings:
    a. "Minnesota Polka," "Gary's Polka," "Mountaineer Polka," "Happy Fellow," and "Meisner Magic," from *Deep Polka: Dance Music from the Midwest* (available from www.folkways.si.edu)
    b. "Sweet Sixteen Polka" and "In Heaven There Is No Beer," from *Deeper Polka: More Dance Music from the Midwest* (available from www.folkways.si.edu)
2. Video:
    a. "Tick Tock Polka" featuring the Al Yankovic Band (www.youtube.com)
    b. "Frank Yankovic on the Johnny Carson Show" (www.youtube.com)
3. Maps of Europe and the United States

### Procedures

1. Find a map Europe, and note regions in Central Europe (especially Bohemia [in the Czech Republic], Poland, Germany, and Slovakia) in which polka has been a strong dance tradition for centuries. Then find the regions in the United States—areas near Chicago, Milwaukee, Minneapolis, Cleveland, and Pittsburgh—where the polka tradition is alive and well.
2. Play examples of polka, American-style, one after another. Identify the instrumentation of the polka bands featured on the selections:

    "Minnesota Polka" (trumpets, tuba, accordion, drums)
    "Gary's Polka" (accordion, tuba, banjo, drums)
    "Mountaineer Polka" (accordion, violin, trumpets, drums)
    "Happy Fellow" (accordion, trumpets, drums)
    "Meisner Magic" (accordion, banjo, saxophone, drums)
    "Sweet Sixteen Polka" (accordion, saxophone, banjo, drums)
    "In Heaven There Is No Beer" (accordion, violin, drums)

3. Listen to the recorded selections again, challenging students to discern the meter of polka music by tapping the pulse and finding the first, accented pulse of each pulse-group. The discussion should lead to the duple meter of polka music that may be heard and felt as "1–2–3–4" or as "1–2."
4. In yet another listening to the selections, have students try these patting and clapping patterns (patting on their laps or on a table/desk surface, clapping hands together). Write the patterns on the board, and on cue to a num-

This lesson was prepared by Patricia Shehan Campbell.

ber, have them change to that pattern as the music plays on. If students become confused, return to clapping only the first pattern (1a) (see figure 3.10).

| Beats | 1 | 2 | 3 | 4 |
|-------|-----|-------|-------|------|
| (1)   | /   | /     | /     | /    |
| (a)   | clap | clap | clap  | clap |
| (b)   | pat  | clap | clap  | clap |
|       |      |      |       |      |
| (2)   | (rest) | /  | /     | /    |
| (a)   | —    | clap | clap  | clap |
| (b)   | —    | pat  | pat   | clap |
|       |      |      |       |      |
| (3)   | /    | /    | / /   | /    |
| (a)   | clap | clap | cl-cl | clap |
| (b)   | pat  | pat  | cl-cl | pat  |
|       |      |      |       |      |
| (4)   | / /  | / /  | (rest) | /   |
| (a)   | cl-cl | cl-cl | —   | cl   |
| (b)   | p-p  | cl-cl | ____ | p    |
|       |      |      |       |      |
| (5)   | (rest) | / / | (rest) | / / |
| (a)   | —    | cl-cl | —    | cl-cl |
| (b)   | —    | p-cl | —     | p-cl |

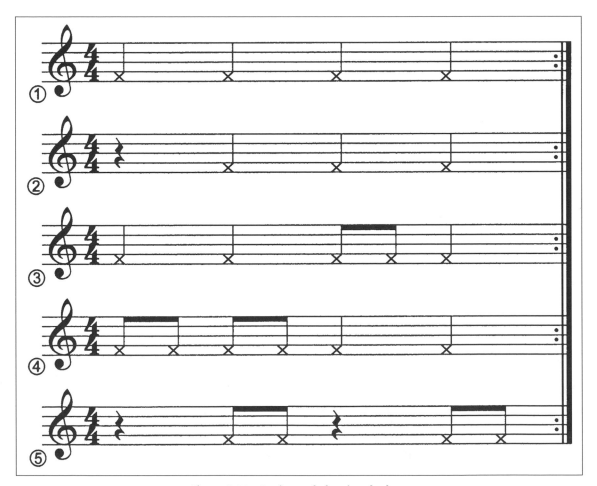

**Figure 3.10  Patting and clapping rhythms**

5. Following repeated listenings, students will become familiar with some of the melodies. Encourage them to hum along, or to sing on a neutral syllable such as "loo," "dee," or "mah," the melodies of selected recordings.

6. Play film examples of polka bands and their dancing audiences. Observe the instruments in these bands, the placement of musicians, their manner of dress, and the movements of the polka dancers. Note that Frankie Yankovic, the Cleveland accordionist who led various Slovenian bands, was a Grammy-award-winner. He was very popular in his time (especially the 1950s through the 1980s) and was known as "the Polka King."

7. Invite a polka dancer as artist-in-residence to demonstrate and teach the movements of a polka dance.

8. Invite an accordionist into classes, particularly of the polka tradition, so that students can see and hear close up the sound of this principal polka instrument.

## Assessment

1. Identify and describe the sound of polka dance music.
2. Sing melodies with recordings of polka dance music.

## MUSIC ACROSS THE CURRICULUM

The following are some suggestions for extending the study of European traditional music across the curriculum to other classroom learning experiences:

1. Assign students the task of seeking out images of Euro-American culture, including photos of neighborhoods, characteristic foods, musical instruments, singers, instrumentalists, and dancers. Fill a bulletin board or display with these images.
2. Search the Internet for further examples of musical genres identifiable as Euro-American, including Anglo-American folk songs, ballads, fiddle tunes, shape-note singing, bluegrass, Cajun styles, and polka.
3. Learn an instrument of the sort featured in these lessons, such as dulcimer, guitar, fiddle (fiddling style on violin), and accordion.
4. Look into the community, tapping parents and grandparents of students, as well as teaching, clerical, and janitorial staff within schools, to invite those with Euro-American identities to visit classrooms to share aspects of their heritage—a story, song, dance, musical instrument, traditional craft, or even cuisine.
5. Find out the local history and culture of the community in terms of Euro-American strands of influence in government and politics, commerce and industry, and health and education.
6. Seek some stories, to read alone or out loud to a group, that reflect the sensibilities and values of Anglo-Americans, Cajuns, German Americans, Polish Americans, and other Americans of European ancestry who comprise the multicultural composite of the country.
7. Look for local festivals that celebrate European cultures in America, where traditional music, dance, arts and crafts, and foods can be sampled.

## NOTE

1. Download a map of the United States from *National Geographic* (www.nationalgeographic.com/xpeditions/atlas/) and project it on a screen for the students.

## DISCOGRAPHY

*British Traditional Ballads in the Southern Mountains*. Vol. 1. Smithsonian Folkways. Selected Child ballads are featured in this recording by Jean Ritchie.

*The Essential Flatt and Scruggs: 'Tis Sweet to Be Remembered*. Sony. Classic songs by the classic duo, this recording includes the widely known "Foggy Mountain Breakdown."

*From Now On*. Smithsonian Folkways. Michael Doucet, fiddle, and Todd Duke, guitar, play duets from the Cajun tradition, as well as other genres (such as blues) in Cajun style.

*Live Recordings 1963–1980: Off the Record*. Vol. 2. Smithsonian Folkways. Bluegrass musicians Bill Monroe and Doc Watson play ballads on guitar and mandolin.

*Old Harp Singing*. Smithsonian Folkways. Mixed male and female singers perform various selections from the Sacred Harp collection.

*70 Years of Hits. Our Heritage*. Classic Midwestern polka tunes comprise this collection by polka leader Frankie Yankovic, including "Cleveland, the Polka Town."

*The Social Harp: Early American Shape-Note Songs*. Rounder. Songs like "Singing School," "Buonaparte," "Wake Up," "Zion's Walls," Weeping Mary," and "Lisbon" are performed by the Sacred Harp Singers of Georgia and Alabama, led by Hugh McGraw.

## FILMOGRAPHY

*Amazing Grace with Bill Moyers* (DVD). Rounder. Featured performers of the song are Judy Collins, Jessye Norman, Johnny Cash, Jean Ritchie, and the Boys Choir of Harlem.

*American Patchwork: Appalachian Journey* (DVD). Media-Generation. Alan Lomax travels through the Southern Appalachians with sound and visual images of the songs, dances, and religious rituals of the descendants of the Scots-Irish frontier people who keep the traditions of their elders alive.

*American Patchwork: Cajun Country* (DVD). Media-Generation. With the guidance of folklorist Alan Lomax, this film explores Cajun culture's roots, their dances in rural Louisiana, and the traditional tales and songs, with features by Canray Fontenot, Bois Sec Ardoin, Michael Doucet, and Dewey Balfa.

*Awake, My Soul: The Story of the Sacred Harp* (DVD). Awake Productions. This film documents Sacred Harp singing and its history of rebellion and tradition.

*High Lonesome: The Story of Bluegrass Music* (DVD). A 1991 documentary film that frames its historical survey around the life and music of Bill Monroe.

*It's Happiness: A Polka Documentary* (DVD). Stun. This film offers a glimpse of the local polka scene in Pulaski, Wisconsin, with a focus on people who strive to revitalize it.

# BIBLIOGRAPHY

Bohlman, Philip V. *The Study of Folk Music in the Modern World*. Bloomington: Indiana University Press, 1988. An assessment of folk music, including songs and instrumental music, in Europe and America, and the scholarship in ethnomusicology and folk-lore that has helped its collection and analysis.

Broven, John. *South to Louisiana: The Music of the Cajun Bayous*. Gretna, La.: Pelican Publishing Company, 1983. A history of Louisiana's musical styles, including Cajun, zydeco, swamp pop, and New Orleans music.

Campbell, Olive, and Cecil J. Sharp. *English Folk Songs from the Southern Appalachians*. New York: Putnam, 1917. This is a collection of Anglo-American ballads and songs from the Southern Appalachian Mountains.

Campbell, Patricia Shehan. *Tunes and Grooves for Music Education*. Upper Saddle River, N.J.: Pearson, 2008. A collection of notated melodies and rhythms, with cultural contexts and suggested experiences provided, including Anglo-American tunes like "Billy Boy," "Arkansas Traveller," "How Can I Keep from Singing?" "Froggie Went A-Courting," "Old Joe Clark," "Wondrous Love," and "In the Pines."

Cantwell, Robert. *Bluegrass Breakdown: The Making of the Old Southern Sound*. Champaign: University of Illinois Press, 2003. This analytical book on the bluegrass sound offers a comprehensive history from its musical roots forward.

Chase, Richard. *Grandfather Tales*. Boston: Houghton Mifflin, 1948. This collection of stories indigenous to the Southern Appalachian Mountains includes "Sody Sallyraytus."

———. *Old Songs and Singing Games*. New York: Dover Publications, 1972. This is an excellent collection of songs, ballads, carols, folk hymns, rounds, singing games, play-party games, and country dances from the Southern Appalachian Mountains.

Child, Francis James. *The English and Scottish Popular Ballads*. New York: Dover Publications, 1965. This is the classic collection of Child ballads.

Conover, Chris. *Froggie Went A-Courting*. New York: Farrar, Straus, and Giraux, 1986. The book contains both the music for the ballad and the charming illustrations of it.

Erbsen, Wayne. *Rural Roots of Bluegrass: Songs, Stories and History*. Pacific, Mo.: Mel Bay Publications, 2003. The music and people of the Southern Mountain country are explored in this book, along with an interweaving of music and lyrics to ninety-four bluegrass songs.

Greene, Victor. *A Passion of Polka: Old-Time Ethnic Music in America*. Berkeley: University of California Press, 1992. This book chronicles the popularization of old-time ethnic music from the turn of the century to the 1960s, with attention to the craze for international dance music in the polka belt of the Midwestern United States and as far from it as Connecticut and Texas.

Jackson, George Pullen. *White Spirituals in the Southern Uplands*. Hatboro, Penn.: Folklore Associates, 1964. This classic tome, first published in 1933, described the fasola singing tradition of shape-notes in the Deep South, which he referred to as "white spirituals."

Keil, Charles, Angeliki V. Keil, and Dick Blau. *Polka Happiness*. Philadelphia: Temple University Press, 1992. This is an account of the musicians, the fans, and the cultural institutions that keep the polka party going among Polish Americans, with 150 historical and contemporary illustrations. Includes leaders in the polka movement like Frankie Yankovic, Li'l Wally, and Walt Solek.

Lomax, Alan. *American Ballads and Folk Songs*. New York: Macmillan, 1964. The classic collection contains a wide variety of traditional Anglo-American tunes and texts.

Nyhan, Pat, with Brian Rollins and David Babb. *Let the Good Times Roll: A Guide to Cajun and Zydeco Music*. Portland, Me.:Upbeat Books, 1998. A comprehensive guide to Cajun and zydeco recordings, including in print and rare recordings. Commentaries and brief histories on Cajun artists, and an introduction by Michael Doucet.

*The Sacred Harp: The Best Collection of Sacred Songs, Hymns, Odes, and Anthems Ever Offered the Singing Public for General Use*. Breman, Ga.: Sacred Harp Publishing Company, 1991. Over 500 four-part songs, including "Lenox," "New Britain," "Northfield," and "Chester," are presented in shape-notes for singing in choral settings.

Savoy, Ann Allen. *Cajun Music: A Reflection of a People*. Vol. 1. Eunice, La.: Bluebird Press, 1985. A definitive collection of over 100 Cajun songs, transcribed with lyrics, along with interviews with musicians and notes on performance techniques and style.

Seeger, Ruth Crawford. *American Folk Songs for Children*. Garden City, NY: Doubleday, 1948. This collection of songs for young children includes Anglo-American songs from New England, the Appalachians, the Ozarks, and elsewhere.

# 4

# Music of Native Peoples of North America

*Bryan Burton and Kay Edwards*

Long before the arrival of European explorers and settlers, a mosaic of cultures covered the North American continent. Hundreds of tribes, languages, religions, and lifestyles developed among these diverse peoples. At the heart of the Native American culture was music. Songs and dances were central to each facet of life from birth to death, including every occasion—sacred or secular, significant or insignificant—that occurred in the lives of these peoples. Songs and dances were integral parts of ceremonies (worship, healing, hunting, agriculture), social events (dances, courtship), and entertainment. A vast repertoire of stories and songs was transmitted intergenerationally through an oral/aural process from the most distant past to the present-day descendants of the original peoples of the western continents. Despite five centuries of subjugation and assimilation during which much of the rich Native American culture—lands, languages, religions, and millions of lives—was lost, this vibrant music continues to not only exist, but to thrive, evolve, and enrich the lives of both the First Americans and the New Americans.

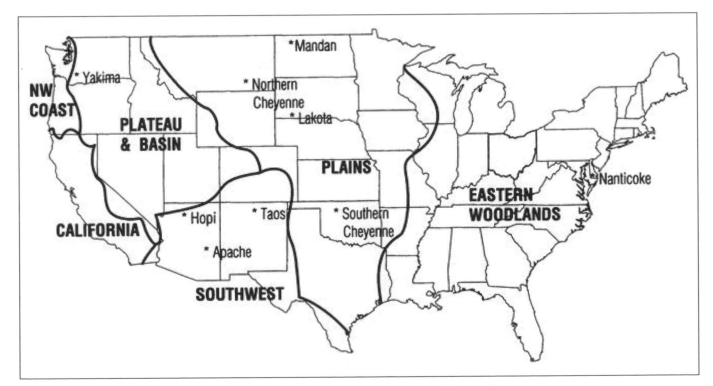

**Figure 4.1   Historical regions of Native American music**

To speak of Native music as a single style is to ignore the richness and diversity of musical expressions found among the Native Peoples. Historically, Native music within the United States and Canada is divided into several general stylistic regions differentiated by such factors as vocal style, song forms, types of instruments, song accompaniments, and type and form of ceremonial music and dance. Traditionally, these regions (shown in figure 4.1) are labeled Eastern Woodlands sometimes divided into Northeastern and Southeastern styles), Plains (often divided into Northern and Southern styles), Great Basin and Plateau, Northwest Coast, California, Arctic, and Southwest (usually divided into Pueblo and Apachean styles). Over time, interaction among tribes, relocation of Native Peoples through government edicts, and recorded music broadcast on radio and television have blurred these once clear stylistic boundaries. Figure 4.2 identifies some of the general characteristics of each style and provides examples that may be downloaded from an Internet source.

Music is functional in this culture, serving to connect the natural and the supernatural through the spiritual power of the music and dance with specific roles assigned to instruments or unique dances. Among the functions served by music in Native cultures are religious ceremonies; healing ceremonies; work songs; game songs; songs to bring success in hunting, war, or agriculture; songs to honor worthy individuals; courting songs; storytelling; and social songs and dances. Although great latitude is allowed when performing social and game songs, ceremonial songs must be performed perfectly in order to ensure a successful outcome of the ceremony. Historically, many songs and dances were performed exclusively by a specific person or group; there were songs exclusively for men, exclusively

**Figure 4.2. Regional styles traits**

| Region | Representative Tribes | Style Traits |
|---|---|---|
| Eastern Woodlands | *Micmac, Nanticoke, Seneca, Mohawk, Cherokee, Narragansett, Penobscot* | Relaxed voices in medium and high ranges; vocal shake/pulsing at ends of phrases; use of call-and-response form; agricultural themes of hunting and raising crops frequently used in lyrics; some use of song cycles; great variety of rhythmic accompaniment on drums, including instances of syncopation; instruments such as small hand drums, water drums, rattles made of turtle shell, cow horn, and bark |
| Plains | *Absarokee (Crow), Dakota, Lakota, Kiowa, Comanche, Cheyenne, Mandan* | Tense, tight, and strained vocal style; northern tribes prefer a high vocal range; southern tribes prefer a medium vocal range; melodies frequently begin high, drop dramatically over the course of the song, and end with repetitions of tonal center; rapid changes in pitch and volume; note pulsations frequently occur; "trills" produced by rapidly fluttering the tongue against the roof of the mouth; sing mostly in unison; one large drum played by several people accompanies the music; use flutes and whistles; bells, shells, and other attachments produce ambient musical sounds |
| Great Basin–Plateau | *Ute, Paiute, Washoe, Bannock, Yakima, Nez Perce, Shoshone* | Vocal style similar to Plains except lower in pitch; simple accompaniments; melodious, frequent use of melodic rise |
| California | *Diegueno, Mojave, Yurok, Pomo, Miwok, Yokut* | Vocal range usually low with a relaxed style; mostly solo singing with occasional examples of polyphony in northern regions; frequent use of rattles and rasps |
| Northwest Coast | *Salish, Haida, Tlingit, Kwakiutl, Chinookans, Suquamish, Skagit, Snohomish* | Complex percussion rhythms; eloquently staged dramas feature song, dance, and carved masks with moving parts; drums include slit boxes and hollowed logs; some instances of polyphony; complex song forms and melodies may include chromatic intervals; some upward keys change as melodies progress |
| Southwest Pueblo | *Hopi, Zuni, Acoma, Santa Clara, Taos, Laguna, Tewa, Tigua* | Vocal style similar to Plains, with lower range and "growling" timbre; melodies lengthy and complex; frequent vocal tension and pulsation; drum sizes vary; each drum played by one person; most singing done in unison; most rituals directed toward agriculture and crop cycles |
| Southwest Apachean | *Navajo, Apache (including Chiricahua, Mescalero, White Mountain, San Carlos, Jicarilla)* | Light, nasal singing style; mixed vocal ranges; frequent use of natural overtone series in melodic structure (with microtonal variations); singing done mostly in unison, but some responsorial songs; occasional use of flutes and whistles; use of Apache violin (made from the agave plant), sole stringed instrument indigenous to North America; drums, water drums, rasps, and bullroarers used as accompaniment; practice elaborate multiday ceremonials incorporating singing, chanting, and sandpainting guided by highly trained practitioners |

for women, or for performance by both men and women. In contemporary Native American society, these once-strict distinctions are beginning to relax, and performances at tribal fairs and powwows are increasingly performed by mixed gender groups.

Song lyrics may be in a Native language, English, vocables, or any combination of these. Although the meanings and functions of vocables have been widely debated, the currently preferred definition of vocables is "meaningful syllables without a clear translation into language."

## INSTRUMENTS

The most familiar instruments in Native American music are the drums and rattles used to accompany song and dance. Other percussion instruments include a variety of rasps, large sticks used to play rhythmic patterns, and bells. The best known melodic instrument is the Native American flute, which has crossed over into Western popular and symphonic music and may be heard in film and television scores as well as on hundreds of recordings from the most traditional styles through new age, rock, and even hip-hop.

A variety of smaller whistles, including the eagle bone whistle are used in both social and ceremonial music. Native American stringed instruments include the Apache violin made from the stalk of the century plant. (This is the only indigenous string instrument—other fiddles and harps are derived from European models.) In the southwestern United States and northwestern Mexico, the European violin has been adapted in a folk instrument used by, among others, the Yaqui, Tarahumara, Tohono O'Odham, and Akmiel O'Odham in both religious and popular settings.

Drums are constructed in many sizes and shapes from such diverse materials as logs, pottery, baskets, animal skins, and metal. Many traditions equate the drumbeat with the heartbeat of Mother Earth or as a means of communication with supernatural powers. In contemporary powwows and tribal fairs, the term "drum" refers not only to the instrument, but also to the performers who play it and sing. Strict codes of conduct are followed by musicians gathered as part of the "drum." The drum used in powwows is often as large as a Western bass drum and is usually held in place on a special frame or stand.

The barrel and frame drums made of wood and animal hide from the Southwest and Plains traditions are the best known of Native drums. However, water drums may be found among Eastern Woodlands tribes as well as Apache and Navajos of the Southwest. In both areas, a varying amount of water is placed in the drum and a wetted skin is stretch across the top until a desired pitch is reached. Slit log drums, large log drums, and box drums are found among the peoples along the Northwest Coast, Alaska, and Arctic areas of Canada.

Rattles display the great inventiveness of Native Peoples in creating instruments from any possible material. Materials may include gourds, turtle shells, rawhide, animal horns, deer hooves, tobacco can lids, discarded metal cans, snake rattles, bird beaks, sea shells, cocoons—every type of material imaginable.

Historically, flutes and whistles were most commonly associated with Native Peoples of the Plains (courting traditions) and Southwest (healing and social music). This tradition was nearly extinct when Doc Tate Navaquaya made a series of recordings in the early 1940s on instruments he had found in various attics and museums. From this work has sprung a thriving traditional of flute playing among nearly all contemporary tribes.

Native American flutes are constructed from a wide range of materials based on local traditions and individual preference. Cedar is preferred by many flute makers and players, but flutes have also been made of bamboo, cane, metal, ceramic, and bone. Typically, the tube is hollowed into two chambers separated by a blockage near the tip of the instrument. The air is diverted over this blockage, outside of the body of the instrument, and back into the lower chamber through an air channel carved into an external decoration referred to as the "bird." Pitches are changed by covering and uncovering tone holes, which range in number from three to six. Pitches may be shaded by finger and breath manipulation to create an infinite variety of sounds. "Dakota Love Song," performed by Robert Tree Cody, is representative of traditional style playing and may be accessed as track 5 on the *American Indian Sampler iMix* (see discography).

The Apache violin is unique among Native instruments and is the only stringed instrument indigenous to North America. This instrument is made from a section of stalk from the century plant (a type of agave); tone holes are carved at appropriate points and one or two strings are placed lengthwise across the top of the instrument. The bow is constructed from a bent willow branch with horsehair attached. The Apache violin is used in social dances, healing, and courtship. Geronimo, known among his own Apache people as a healer, prophet, and musician was one of the craftsmen to make this instrument. One of his instruments is in the Peabody Museum. The best known contemporary maker of the Apache violin, Chesley Goseyun Wilson, a singer, healer, actor, and artist, has been honored with a Heritage Fellowship Award from the National Endowment for the Arts, among other honors. He made a set of Apache violins for use by the Kronos Quartet in performing Brent Michael Davids' quartet, "Mtukwekok Naxkomao" ("The

Singing Woods"). An example of Chesley's performance is "I'll Go with You" on *The Wood That Sings*, which may be downloaded from www.folkways.si.edu. The Apache violin tradition may be further explored in *When the Earth Was Like New* (Wilson, Wilson, and Burton, 1994).

Another stringed instrument tradition, dating back to the seventeenth century, exists among several tribes, including Yaqui, Tarahumara, Tohono O'Odham, Akmiel O'Odham, and several Rio Grande Pueblos, in the southwestern United States and northern Mexico. Native artisans originally copied European instruments—violins, harps, and vihuelas—brought by missionaries, but the designs, individual natures of the instruments, and musical usages have long since transformed these instruments into an authentic folk form. Such instruments are used in social and popular dances including the waila ("chicken scratch") style of southern Arizona as well as in religious and ceremonial dances such as the pascola and Fiesta Gloria among the Yaquis and Matachines dances through the region. A pascola dance, "Mamna Cialim" ("Green Spinach"), may be heard on track 15 of the *American Indian Sampler iMix* (see resources).

## THE INTERTRIBAL POWWOW

The modern intertribal powwow grew out of the tribal fairs, family gatherings, and entertainment performances such as those promoted by Fred Harvey for passengers of the Santa Fe Railway and Buffalo Bill's Wild West Show. Because many tribes—particularly those on the East Coast—have lost cultural elements including language, religion, song, and dance as a result of generations of assimilation and relocation, an intertribal style of song and dance developed based, in large part, on the Plains style songs learned from Native American performers traveling with circuses and wild west shows during the early twentieth century. Other Plains influences grew from the closeness of tribes, originally from throughout the United States, now crammed onto reservations in Indian Territory (Oklahoma).

Today's powwow serves as a contemporary gathering place for all Native Peoples to celebrate their identity and to promote Native culture. These gatherings also provide a forum for discussions of Native rights, health and educational concerns, and other sociopolitical issues. Music and dance are the centerpiece of these occasions. Typically, a powwow begins with a grand entry featuring dancers of all Nations and dancing styles. After an invocation or flag song, the powwow continues long into the evening with competitive dancing mixed with social dances, honor dances, and specialty dances (such as a hoop dance) unique to a particular tribal tradition. Among the most common dances are Men's Fancy Dance, Women's Fancy Shawl Dance, Men's Traditional Dance, Women's Traditional Dance, intertribal dances, and so on. These dances and their songs are more fully described in Diamond's *Native American Music in Northeast North America* and the second edition of Burton's *Moving within the Circle: Contemporary Native American Music and Dance*. *A Dancing People* explores the cultural context and historical background of powwow dancing.

## CONTEMPORARY NATIVE AMERICAN MUSIC

Musical taste and style are as diverse among Native Americans as among the remainder of American society. In addition to preserving music from past generations, contemporary singers such as the Black Lodge Singers (see track 25 of the *American Indian Sampler iMix*) create new songs in these traditional styles. New age, jazz, country, rock, reggae, hip-hop, and more have been formed by musicians from all tribal backgrounds and Native composers are also actively producing symphonic works, including ballets, chamber works, and operas. A growing number of Native composers are now producing music for television and motion picture scores.

Some Native musicians, however, do not incorporate elements of Native American music or began their careers in Western popular music before returning to their musical roots. This list includes Robbie Robertson (rhythm guitarist for The Band), Rita Coolidge, and Buffy Saint Marie. Native descendants who do not typical identify themselves as Native American, including Wayne Newton, Cher, and Johnny Cash, have also had successful popular careers.

Native Americans using popular genres have created syncretic styles that incorporate elements of both Native American and Western popular musics. For example, instruments may include Native American drums, rattles, and flutes in addition to the drum sets, keyboards and guitars of contemporary popular styles. Missionary hymns (listen to "One Drop of Blood" performed by the National Cherokee Children's Choir available from iTunes), radio broadcasts, and recordings brought Western styles into contact with Native musicians and the fusion began and continues grow. Tom Bee, now a major record producer for rising young Native musicians, founded the first commercially successful Native rock band XIT (Crossing of Indian Tribes) in the 1970s with such well-known Native performers as Keith Secola, Robert Mirabal, Jim Boyd (a former member of XIT), Red Thunder, flutists R. Carlos Nakai and Robert

**Table 4.1. Contemporary Native American Music**

| Genre | Artist | Selection | Album |
|---|---|---|---|
| Rock | Tom Bee and XIT | "Christopher Columbus" | *Without Reservation* |
| Blues | Keith Secola | "Kokopelli Blues" | *Native Americana* |
| Big Band | Murray Porter | "1492 Who Found Who" | *1492 Who Found Who* |
| New Age | Brule | "Seven Generations" | *Star People* |
| Rap/Hip Hop | Robbie Bee & The Boyz from the Rez | "Let's Save Our Mother Earth" | *Reservation of Education* |
| Contemporary Folk | Joanne Shenandoah | "You Can Hear Them Dancing" | *Once in a Red Moon* |
| Reggae | Native Roots | "Frybread" | *Rain Us Love* |
| Country | Michael Trailwalker Wilson | "Custer" | *Native Country* |
| Women's Vocal Ensemble | Ulali | "Going Home" | *Heartbeat: Voices of First Nations' Women* |
| Christian Hymn | Cherokee National Children's Choir | "One Drop of Blood" | *Voices of the Creator's Children* |
| Orchestral | R. Carlos Nakai | "Two World Concerto II" | *Two World Concerto* |
| Contemporary Orchestral | Brent Michael Davids | "Indians Win Again" | *Bright Circle* |
| Motion Picture | Buffy Saint Marie | "Up Where We Belong" | *Up Where We Belong* |
| Easy Rock | Robert Mirabal | "The Dance" | *Music from a Painted Cave* |

Tree Cody, and Bee's son Robbie, following in his footsteps. The typical contemporary Native American musical work incorporates Native sociopolitical themes as well as elements of traditional music.

Contemporary Native American life is extraordinarily diverse and encompasses every sound and style of music performed on the North American continent. Despite evolution of style and use of contemporary sounds and techniques, Native musicians keep "one foot planted firmly in tradition," placing an indelibly Native American stamp upon these modern musics.

Listen to the examples in table 4.1 to explore many of the sounds and styles of contemporary Native American music. All examples may be downloaded from the iTunes store.

## LESSON 1: "BEAR DANCE," CHEROKEE ANIMAL DANCE

### National Standard

- Listening to, analyzing, and describing music—(e) respond through purposeful movement to selected prominent music characteristics or to specific musical events while listening to music

### Objectives

Students will:

1. be able to describe or trace melodic pattern;
2. be able to perform appropriate movements to distinguish between phrases of "Bear Dance";
3. optional: students will be able to play one note per beat on a Native American hand drum.

### Materials

1. Recording of "Bear Dance" (may be found on the Native American Resources page at www.singingcanaries.com or found in *Moving within the Circle*, 2nd ed.)
2. Transcription of "Bear Dance" (see figure 4.3)
3. Optional: Native American hand drums or appropriate substitutes
4. Optional: Story "How Bears Came into Being" (*Moving within the Circle*, 2nd ed., or download from "Native American Resources" at www.singingcanaries.com)

### Procedures

1. Introduce "Bear Dance" to students through a brief discussion of the importance of animal dances in Native culture (honoring the animal for its importance to the culture) and, if time permits, tell a story about bears, such as "How Bears Came into Being," which explains origins of bears and their movements.
2. Either sing or play recording of "Bear Dance," asking students to trace melody in the air with their hands.
3. After song has been played/sung, invite students to describe the melodic pattern for the first phrase of the song (on same pitch throughout) and second phrase of song (begins high and moves lower).
4. Explain that mimicking actions of the bear while dancing is an important way in which Native Americans honor the bear for its importance to the people. Invite descriptions of different movements bears might make.
5. Invite students to select which actions are "high" movements and which are "low" movements.

**Figure 4.3   Transcription of "Bear Dance"**

**Table 4.2.  Lesson 1 Assessment**

| Student performs "low" movements during first phrase: | | |
| --- | --- | --- |
| Always | Sometimes | Seldom |

| Student performs "high" movements during second phrase: | | |
| --- | --- | --- |
| Always | Sometimes | Seldom |

OPTIONAL
| Student plays one note per beat on hand drum: | | |
| --- | --- | --- |
| Always | Sometimes | Seldom |

6. Instruct students to perform low movements during first phrase of song and high movements during second phrase. (Remember that song repeats numerous times on the recording.) Students will perform movements while taking one step to each beat. Optional: If movement space is limited in classroom, assign a number of students to play a steady pulse on Native American hand drums. On subsequent repeats of this step, allow students to switch with other students to allow each student to both move or play.

7. Summarize and review lesson, inviting student comments on class success.

## Assessment

Observe students as they perform movements to a recording or a live performance of a song, noting whether they correctly match high and low movements to phrase and take one step to each beat. Optional: If students are assigned to play drums, note whether they are successful in playing a steady pulse (see table 4.2).

## Cross-Curricular Connections: Literature

Teacher may select a bear story to include as a storytelling activity in which students may dramatize the story. There are many collections of Native American stories that include not only stories about bears, but also stories about many animals. "Why We Have Night and Day" (*When the Earth Was Like New*) is an Apache story that tells the origins of characteristics of many familiar animals.

## LESSON 2: "O HAL'LWE," NANTICOKE WOMEN'S HONORING DANCE

### National Standards

- Singing, alone or with others, a varied repertoire of music; (c) sing, from memory, a varied repertoire of songs representing genres and styles from diverse cultures
- Listening to, analyzing, and describing music; (a) identify simple music forms when presented aurally
- Understanding music in relation to history and culture; (c) identify various uses of music in their daily experiences and describe characteristics that make certain music suitable for each use

### Objectives

Students will:

1. identify call-and-response form in "O Hal'Lwe";
2. perform call-and-response in "O Hal'Lwe";
3. demonstrate an understanding of the historical and cultural significance of "O Hal'Lwe."

### Materials

1. Transcription of "O Hal'Lwe" (see figure 4.4)
2. Recording of "O Hal'Lwe," available on Native American Resources page at www.singingcanaries.com
3. Native American drum (hand drum or powwow drum) or appropriate substitute
4. Map of State of Delaware

**Figure 4.4   Transcription of "O Hal'Lwe"**

## Procedures

1. Provide a brief cultural and historical background for "O Hal'Lwe."
   a. Show location of Nanticoke lands in Delaware.
   b. Explain that Nanticoke people were encountered by European explorers in the 1580s and most were forced to abandon their lands due to a number of failed treaties. Although many moved to Pennsylvania and New York, a few families remained on traditional lands, masking their Native identity by assuming the role of "Free Colored." In recent years, the Nanticoke have reasserted their cultural identity, established a tribal museum, and obtained state recognition as Native Americans. The Nanticoke host an annual powwow on traditional lands in Delaware each fall.
   c. Discuss the role of women among the Nanticoke. Women traditionally managed affairs of the tribe, owned the property, and were honored by the tribe's cultural heritage.
   d. Explain significance of "O Hal'Lwe." Although most of the Nanticoke language has been lost, the words "O Hal'Lwe" have been preserved in this song. "O Hal'Lwe" refers to the mighty oak tree and compares the role of women in their culture to the oak tree that brings forth new life and provides shelter and protection as each new generation grows to maturity. Traditionally, men drum and sing this song while the women—often many generations of the same family—dance together as a demonstration of multigenerational bonding.
1. Play recording or sing "O Hal'Lwe," requesting that students identify the form of the song (AB, call-and-response) by raising hands when singing changes from solo to group.
2. Teach the song phrase by phrase. Note that although only men traditionally sing this song, for educational purposes, all students will learn the song.
3. Assign selected students to play drum accompaniment (even eighth notes) and have class sing "O Hal'Lwe."
4. Teach the dance. Note that although traditionally only women perform the dance, for educational purposes, all students will learn the dance.
   a. Form a large circle, facing clockwise.
   b. During the call: Dancers move forward stepping on the ball of the foot (the heel never touches the ground) with a pulse on each half beat.
   c. During the response: Each dancer rotates in a small clockwise circle returning to face the original direction by end of response. the original direction
   d. Resume forward motion, and so on.
5. Review and summarize lesson inviting student comments and student assessment of performance.

## Assessment

1. Teacher notes student responses in discussion, questioning, and review of historical background (see table 4.3).
2. Teacher notes student response to form when "O Hal'Lwe" is aurally presented.
3. Teacher listens to singing, playing, and observes dancing.

**Table 4.3. Lesson 2 Assessment**

| Student demonstrates understanding of historical background by answering teacher questions | | |
|---|---|---|
| Always | Sometimes | Seldom |

| Student is able to sing assigned part (call/response) with accurate pitches, rhythms, and lyrics | | |
|---|---|---|
| Always | Sometime | Seldom |

| Student is able to play drum accompaniment as assigned | | |
|---|---|---|
| Always | Sometimes | Seldom |

| Student is able to perform dance accurately | | |
|---|---|---|
| Always | Sometimes | Seldom |

## LESSON 3: "NDN KAR," CONTEMPORARY ROUND DANCE SONG

### National Standards

- Listening to, analyzing, and describing music; (a) analyze aural examples of a varied repertoire of music, representing genres and cultures, by describing the uses of elements of music and expressive devices
- Understanding music in relation to history and culture; (e) identify and describe music genres and styles that show the influence of two or more cultural traditions, identify the cultural source of each influence, and trace the historical conditions that produced the synthesis of influences

### Objectives

Students will:

1. identify verse and chorus sections of "NDN KAR" (AB form);
2. identify Western and Native American influences such as instruments, melodic design, and language in "NDN KAR";
3. demonstrate an understanding of the way in which this synthesis developed;
4. optional: Native American hand drums and rattles or acceptable classroom substitute.

### Materials

1. Recording of "NDN KAR" (Keith Secola on *Circle*, downloadable from iTunes)
2. Lesson 3 Worksheet
3. In-class computer, projection devices, etc., appropriate for Internet access and display

### Procedures

1. Provide brief background on Keith Secola and "NDN KAR."

   a. Visit www.secola.com and project site for classroom viewing.
   b. Have students read the "Biography" page to discover educational background of Keith Secola, to identify musical influences, and examine history of his musical life including major awards and other recognition.

2. Play "NDN KAR" for class asking students to identify chorus and verse sections of song by raising hand when change occurs. Alternately, have students identify changes by noting time in minutes and seconds.
3. Lead class discussion, inviting students to comment upon the mixture of Western and Native American elements.
4. Distribute Lesson 3 Worksheet (table 4.4); then play the recording again, asking students to identify specific uses of elements from each culture within sections of the song.
5. Invite students to discuss the mixture of elements and, drawing from information discovered on www.secola.com, determine specific influences that might have resulted in this fusion of styles.
6. Optional: Play "NDN KAR" a third time, allowing selected students to play Native American drums to provide underlying rhythmic patterns. How does this rock pattern relate to traditional Native American drum rhythms?

**Table 4.4.   Lesson 3 Worksheet**

|                              | Native American | Western Popular |
|------------------------------|-----------------|-----------------|
| Lyrics—Chorus                |                 |                 |
| Lyrics—Verse                 |                 |                 |
| Melodic Structure—Chorus     |                 |                 |
| Melodic Structure—Verse      |                 |                 |
| Vocal Style—Chorus           |                 |                 |
| Vocal Style—Verse            |                 |                 |
| Instruments                  |                 |                 |

## Assessment

1. Teacher collects Lesson 3 Worksheet and reviews student responses (tables 4.5 and 4.6).
2. Optional: Student is able to play correct underlying percussion pattern.

## Optional Extension

Secola has recorded many versions of this song in a variety of musical styles from blues, to somewhat techno, to instrumental versions for a film score. Download or obtain several versions of this tune (examples: "Son of Indian Car" on *Wild Band of Indians*, "Millennium Cars" on *Fingermonkey*, and "NDN KARZ 49" on *Native Americana—a Coup Stick*) and compare the arrangements, lyrics, cultural elements, etc. Make a comparison chart showing style, influences, instrumentation, and so forth.

## Cross-Curricular Connection: Social Studies

The lyrics of "NDN KAR" are a social commentary about contemporary Native American life: high unemployment on reservations, high poverty levels, alcoholism, illiteracy, and racial profiling. However, Secola places these issues in a humorous story about a dilapidated automobile with rusty plates, faulty engine, and screaming radio that is held together only by a bumper sticker reading "Indian Power." Secola states that he uses humor as a teaching tool and a weapon to fight for his culture. "If I was to raise my fist and shout about these things, nobody would listen. Humor causes them to listen, enjoy, and then think about the issues."[1] Play "NDN KAR" and invite students to identify lyrics that address specific sociopolitical issues. Investigate (online and in print) statistics on the issues listed above. Organize a class discussion on contemporary Native American life on reservations.

**Table 4.5.  Lesson 3 Student Review**

| | | |
|---|---|---|
| Student correctly identifies cultural source of lyrics in chorus | YES | NO |
| Student correctly identifies cultural source of lyrics in verse | YES | NO |
| Student correctly identifies melodic structure of chorus | YES | NO |
| Student correctly identifies melodic structure of  verse | YES | NO |
| Student correctly identifies cultural source of vocal style (chorus) | YES | NO |
| Student correctly identifies cultural source of vocal style (verse) | YES | NO |
| Student identifies at least two Native American instruments used in NDN KAR | YES | NO |
| Student identifies at least three western rock instruments used in NDN KAR | YES | NO |

**Table 4.6.  Lesson 3 Student Worksheet: Possible Answers**

| | Native American | Western Popular |
|---|---|---|
| Lyrics—Chorus | Vocables | |
| Lyrics—Verse | | English |
| Melodic Structure—Chorus | Collapsible melody | |
| Melodic Structure—Verse | | Western popular |
| Vocal Style—Chorus | Tense, Plains style | |
| Vocal Style—Verse | | Western rock |
| Instruments | Rattles, hand drums | Guitar, electric bass, keyboard, drum set |

## LESSON 4: "MOCCASIN GAME SONG," APACHE

**National Standards**

- Singing, alone and with others, a varied repertoire of music; (c) sing from memory a varied repertoire of songs representing genres and styles from diverse cultures
- Performing on instruments, alone or with others, a varied repertoire of music; (a) perform on pitch, in rhythm, with appropriate dynamics and timbre, and maintain a steady tempo; (f) perform independent parts while other students sing or play contrasting parts
- Understanding music in relation to history and culture; (c) identify various uses of music in their daily experiences and describe characteristics that make certain music suitable for each use

**Objectives**

Students will:

1. sing (and play on recorder—optional) a contemporary version of a "Moccasin Game Song" from the Navajo (Diné) nation;
2. understand the song's meaning and purpose (to accompany the game);
3. play a simplified version of the game and learn its cultural significance/context.

**Materials**

1. Sets of four small moccasins (can use moccasin-style suede child-size slippers from a retail store as substitutes); for extra sets, use shoes or other containers such as small paper cups
2. A small stone for each set of four moccasins

**Figure 4.5   Transcription of "Moccasin Game Song" (Navajo)**

3. Recordings of moccasin game songs (tracks 3 and 4 from *Native American Samples iMix* [see discography]; track 3 contains several moccasin games songs while track 4 is a contemporary song)
4. Recorders (optional)
5. Non-pitched percussion (hand drums, Indian rattles, or maraca substitutes)

## Procedures

1. Provide historical and cultural background about the moccasin game: Explain that you have a special song that has a story and a game with it from the Navajo nation. Ask if students know who the Navajo are. Tell the class that the Navajo call themselves Diné (The People). Point out that the Navajo Reservation is the largest reservation in the United States and that it is primarily in northeastern Arizona and northwestern New Mexico. Locate the Navajo Reservation on a map. Show photos of the reservation and its people, in both traditional and contemporary clothing, using books such as *A New True Book: The Navajo* by Alice Osinski (Children's Press, Chicago) and other sources.
2. Listen to "Moccasin Game Song" from track 4 of the *American Indian Samples iMix* (see figure 4.5, set in a different key) while softly patting a half-note steady beat. Use simple hand movement to designate the pitch movement.
3. Sing the melody; have students echo while patting the beat softly.
4. Do the same for the descant. Put parts together. Learn parts on recorder (optional).
5. Learn the second melody (on recorder—optional), written out in 6/4, while softly clapping the quarter-note pulse with a two-finger clap. Put this together with the first melody. Put half-note pulse together with quarter-note pulse; transfer to hand drums and rattles if desired.
6. Introduce the legend and game (see below), including when the legend/story would be told (wintertime only—we show respect by only teaching this lesson in the wintertime).
7. Ask for eight volunteers to play the game, four to a team (the number four is very significant to American Indian tribes). Have other students sing and play their recorders/percussion instruments (or use body percussion). One team is "it" and someone from that team gets to hide the pebble in a moccasin, while its members try to distract the opposing team, who try to keep track of which moccasin the pebble has been placed within; at the end (or when you stop) they indicate which moccasin they think contains the pebble/rock. Rotate game players and instrument players.
8. Set up additional teams of players. If desired, all can play the game while just listening to the recording. Ask if this sounds like a traditional or contemporary version of a moccasin game song (contemporary in that it uses guitar, however, the melody is traditional). Ask for further description. Compare the recording to the more traditional moccasin game songs on track 3. Note that a woman (Sharon Burch) is singing on the contemporary version along with a man (A. Paul Ortega), while the traditional versions feature only male singers. If possible, show photographs of Sharon Burch and A. Paul Ortega.
9. Closure: Ask students to tell the class what Indian nation we learned about today and something about them, to describe the legend behind the game and song. Point out how connected the story, game, and song are and that this interconnectedness (integration) is very common and important in Indian cultures.

## Assessment

1. Check for vocal accuracy with good tone; check for the ability to sing in two-part harmony.
2. Check for beat competency for macro- and micro-beat.
3. Check for understanding and respect of the story, game, and cultural elements.

## Music across the Curriculum: Literature

Seek stories related to the moccasin game among various Native Peoples and use in storytelling to enhance performance of the game as students dramatize the story. A brief version of an Apache version of the story is provided below by Kay Edwards. A more complete version of the story may be found in *When the Earth Was Like New: Western Apache Stories and Songs*.

## The Shoe Game Legend

The shoe game played by the Navajo people during the winter is something the animals back in the first world played to determine whether to have all daytime or all nighttime. All of the night animals teamed up against the day animals to play the game. The game started with all of the animals' shoes stuck in the dirt, and they hid a yucca seed inside one of their shoes. The object of the game was to let the opposite team guess in which shoe the yucca seed was hidden. The team with the most correct guesses would then get to choose whether to have continuous day or continuous night.

The Owl was determined to have the night animals win, so he decided to cheat and not hide the seed in a shoe; instead, he held the yucca seed in his claw. As dawn approached, the night animals were winning, but one of the day animals noticed what had happened, hit the Owl's claw, and the seed came rolling out. Then the sun came up.

As the sun rose, the Bear, who was sleeping, was caught by the rays of the sun as it hit his back, which gave him the rust color of his coat. Because he was not fully awake, he put his shoes on backwards, and to this day, you can tell that his shoes are still on backwards.

The Rabbit was also caught by the sun as its rays came through the woods, and as the sun's rays touched the lower half of the Rabbit's body, they gave his fur a yellowish tint, which we can still see today.

Because neither side really won, the world enjoys both day and night.

## LESSON 5: "HO HO WATANAY," IROQUOIS LULLABY

**National Standards**

- Singing, alone and with others, a varied repertoire of music; (c) sing from memory a varied repertoire of songs representing genres and styles from diverse cultures
- Listening to, analyzing, and describing music; (b) demonstrate perceptual skills by moving, by answering questions about, and by describing aural examples of music of various styles representing diverse cultures
- Understanding music in relation to history and culture; (c) identify various uses of music in their daily experiences and describe characteristics that make certain music suitable for each use

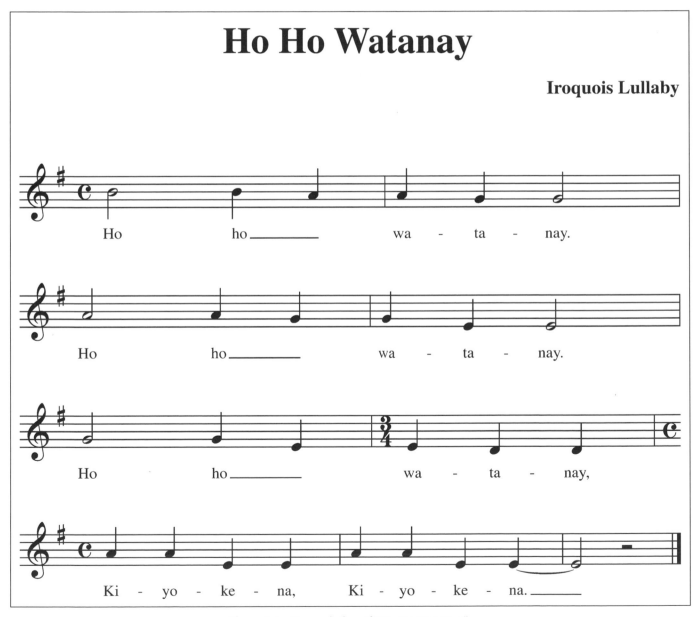

**Figure 4.6   Transcription of "Ho Ho Watanay"**

## Objectives

Students will:

1. listen, describe, and compare two lullabies;
2. use body motions to rock a baby to the beat;
3. sing a song in Iroquois.

## Materials

1. Recording of "Ho Ho Watanay" from *One Elephant, Deux Elephants* (available from http://play.rhapsody.com/sharonloisandbram/oneelephantdeuxelephants/hohowatanayiroquoislullaby)
2. Recordings of other Native American lullabies such as "Nana's Lullaby" from Mary Youngblood's *Heart of the World* (*American Indian Samples iMix*, track 6), or "Lakota Lullaby" from Robert Tree Cody's *Dreams from the Grandfather* (*American Indian Samples iMix*, track 7)
3. Round stickers of a sleeping child's face for each student, in various colors (white, brown, red, yellow)
4. Any children's book on the Iroquois, such as one from *The New True Book* series

## Procedures

1. Give instructions: "Let's listen to an American Indian lullaby."
   a. Do you think the words will sound like our English words?
   b. Do you think an Indian man or woman would sing just like you or your mom or dad?
   c. Would it be polite to laugh at the way the song sounds?
   d. Let's treat the song as if the person was right here singing for you. . . . Now let's listen.
   e. Locate Iroquois on map of Indian nations; show pictures of the Iroquois such as those in the book *The New True Book: The Iroquois*.
2. Use the lullaby to rock a baby to sleep to the beat of the music (idea borrowed from Barbara Andress). Have each child hold his or her index finger out for you, palm up. Place a sleeping child sticker on each child's finger. Cradle arms and rock to the beat. Then, learn to sing the first song ("Ho Ho Watanay)" while rocking (teach phrase by phrase).
3. Look at pictures of Native American cradleboards, used to hold and carry a baby. Learn to sing the song in a key suitable for children's voices as provided.
4. Teach "Ho Ho Watanay" (see figure 4.6). Note translation of song text: "Oh my little one, oh my little one, oh my little one, Go to sleep, go to sleep."
5. Invite student answers to following questions:
   a. For a baby to fall asleep, would we want to rock it fast or slow?
   b. Hard and rough, or gently and smoothly?
   c. Loud or soft? Now let's listen again.

**Table 4.7.   Observation of Student Responses**

During discussion of culture, student demonstrates understanding and respect

| | | |
|---|---|---|
| Always | Sometimes | Seldom |

Student performs "Ho Ho Wataney" with accurate pitches, rhythms, and lyrics

| | | |
|---|---|---|
| Always | Sometimes | Seldom |

Student maintains a steady beat during the rocking activity

| | | |
|---|---|---|
| Always | Sometimes | Seldom |

**Assessment**

1. Teacher observes and notes student response and performance (table 4.7).

**Optional Extensions**

1. Learn more about the Iroquois Indians; learn another Iroquois song.
2. Listen and compare to a contemporary-style Navajo lullaby such as "Little One" from Sharon Burch's *Yazzie Girl*.
3. Listen and compare to other Native American lullabies such as "Nana's Lullaby" from Mary Youngblood's *Heart of the World* (*American Indian Samples iMix*, track 6), or "Lakota Lullaby" from Robert Tree Cody's *Dreams from the Grandfather* (*American Indian Samples iMix*, track 7).
4. Listen and compare to lullabies from other world cultures. Compare to a well-known lullaby such as "Hush Little Baby."

## LESSON 6: HOPI RATTLE LESSON

### National Standards

- Performing on instruments, alone or with others, a varied repertoire of music; (b) perform easy rhythmic, melodic, and chordal patterns accurately on rhythmic, melodic, and harmonic classroom instruments; (c) perform expressively a varied repertoire of music representing diverse genres and styles
- Listening to, analyzing, and describing music; (b) demonstrate perceptual skills by moving, by answering questions about, and by describing aural examples of music of various styles representing diverse cultures
- Understanding music in relation to history and culture; (b) describe in simple terms how elements of music are used in music examples from various cultures of the world; (c) identify various uses of music in their daily experiences and describe characteristics that make certain music suitable for each use

**Figure 4.7  American Indian symbols**

## Objectives

Students will:

1. play rattles, using appropriate rhythms, to accompany recordings of Hopi traditional and contemporary music;
2. suggest possible meanings of rattle decorations based on a chart of Indian symbols;
3. participate in a cooperative learning environment.

## Materials

1. Four to six assorted Hopi rattles (if authentic rattles are not available, show photos of Hopi rattles and substitute maracas when playing the instruments, explaining that the maracas are typically from Mexico and are not therefore authentic for the music)
2. Listening stations with four to six headphones (optional, one station/group)
3. Page of Indian symbols (four to six copies, one/group) (see figure 4.7)
4. Map of the United States with the location of the Hopi reservation clearly marked (primarily in the northeast corner of Arizona, within the Navajo Reservation)
5. Recording of "Hopi Basket Dance" from *Authentic Music of the American Indian,* (http://phobos.apple.com/WebObjects/MZStore.woa/wa/viewAlbum?i=145409994&id=145406486&s=143441)
6. Personal accounts of the Hopi Basket Dance found on the Internet at www.jayepurplewolf.com/PHOENIX/HOPILORE/hopibasketdance.html and/or www.thenaturalamerican.com/basket_dance_at_old_oraibi.htm (Teacher Resource)
7. Hopi Teen Radio program podcast (free download from http://phobos.apple.com/WebObjects/MZStore.woa/wa/viewPodcast?id=120604948)
8. Recording of "Ya-ha Na Ho-ya" ("Be Strong as a Bear") from *Ideas That Sing* (http://phobos.apple.com/WebObjects/MZStore.woa/wa/viewAlbum?i=254502169&id=254501799&s=143441)

## Procedures

1. Divide students into cooperative learning groups of four students/group, assigning each a role: (a) Reader/Spokesperson; (b) Materials Coordinator, who gets the materials for the group and returns them at the end of the lesson; (c) Secretary; (d) Checker/Encourager, who checks that group members all contribute and provides positive comments to keep the group on task, reach consensus, and can explain why.
2. Explain that American Indian instruments are thought to have a life or spirit in them because they are made from living things; the instruments are very special and must be treated carefully with respect.
3. Allow groups to examine the rattles and discuss possible meanings of the symbols on the rattle; explain that one cannot know the true meanings without asking the artist who made the rattle. Spokesperson for each group reports on the group's ideas to the class.
4. Play the recording of "Hopi Basket Dance" and guide students in hearing the many changes of the rattle/voice part. Show the location of Hopiland on a map. Explain that the Hopi call themselves "Hopitu," or "peaceful ones"; overall, the Hopi nation are a people of peace and spirituality. They are known for kachina (katsina) carvings and dances, jewelry, baskets, pottery, and gourd rattles. Their rattles are used in religious ceremonies as well as in social dance songs, and are used by contemporary musicians of many tribal nations.
5. Have students take turns playing the rattle with the recording.
6. After reading the personal accounts of the Hopi Basket Dance from the Internet, the teacher can summarize for the class. The Basket Dance celebrates the end of harvest and is an annual event. Items are redistributed to help everyone prepare for the winter ahead. The giving of gifts to everyone in the crowd watching the dance is a traditional part of the dances of many Pueblo and other American Indian nations.
7. Optional: Listen to part of the Hopi Teen Radio podcast from Hopi High School. What similar events are happening there on the Hopi Reservation compared to a high school in our neighborhood (sports events, parent-teacher conferences, in-service day for teachers, etc.)? The small groups can discuss, write, and report to the class; or do this altogether as a large group.
8. Optional: If time permits, play the recording of "Ya-ha Na Ho-ya" ("Be Strong as a Bear") and join in singing when the children on the recording do so. This is thought to be a rendition of a Hopi song, and can serve as an example of a contemporary song as compared to the traditional Basket Dance song. If desired, have the group

members take turns adding the rattles to the song as you listen. Note that instead of starting and stopping and going different speeds, this song has a steady beat.

9. Optional: As a separate class project, the teacher can purchase gourds from a local grower and allow the students to make their own gourd rattle, decorate it with symbols that have personal meaning, and use the rattles in a concert along with "Mos' Mos'" ("Hopi Cat Song"), found in basal series music textbooks. For directions and ideas, please e-mail Kay Edwards at KayMusEd@aol.com.

## Assessment

1. Observe individual students to see if they played the rattle with proper technique and could match the rhythms of the recording "all of the time," "some of the time," or "not yet."

2. Check to see if all group members are involved and on task (participate, share ideas, take turns with instrument, encourage one another, respectful of instruments).

3. Check for understanding of Hopi culture and the location of the Hopi Reservation by asking questions based on the lesson.

4. Have each small group discuss the following questions and fill out a simple Cooperative Group Processing sheet indicating if they did "all of the time," "some of the time," or "not enough":

   a. Did everyone contribute ideas?
   b. Did we share our materials?
   c. Did we help and encourage one another?
   d. Did we finish our work in time?

## MUSIC ACROSS THE CURRICULUM

Whenever possible, teachers will want to integrate the study of Native American music with other subject areas, thus helping students begin to develop a broader cultural context for their musical study. Teachers may wish to consider the following suggestions:

1. Develop a bulletin board focusing on the Native American culture. Have the students look for maps and good pictures of the people and their arts and crafts. Copy illustrations of these Native musical instruments and attach them to the map of to the United States or a map showing historical locations of Native American tribes.

2. Invite a Native American to visit the class and share his or her stories, arts and crafts, songs, and descriptions of lifestyles. A university community or Native American cultural center may be able to suggest people who represent various Native American nations, or your students may have friends or family members who would be willing to volunteer. Encourage them to bring artifacts, including art works and musical instruments, from their culture.

3. Many Native American songs are connected to a story drawn from traditional literature. For example, in this chapter, "Bear Dance" is associated with several stories explaining the origin of bears. Other songs may pass along history, social values, or serve as a means of telling a story. Make a connection between music and literature by integrating storytelling into the music lesson. Classroom teachers may wish to follow up the music lesson by including a number of Native American stories in their literature and reading classes.

4. If you live near a tribal center, museum, or reservation, plan a field trip to visit the site and/or to observe a pow-wow or demonstration of tribal arts and crafts in addition to music and dance. Make a connection with science by studying Native use of plants and natural resources.

5. When studying American history, include the Native American perspective in the lessons. Many contemporary Native American songs use specific events or historical personages as subject matter and provide an alternative view of these events and people than is usually presented in history texts. "1492 Who Found Who?" and "Christopher Columbus," for example, offer a Native view of the "discovery" of America.

6. Discuss contemporary films and plays that illustrate the Native American experience such as: *Dances with Wolves*, *Pow-Wow Highway*, *Smoke Signals*, and *Geronimo*. Compare the presentation of the Native American culture with that of earlier generations of films such as *Drums Along the Mohawk*, *The Searchers*, and *Broken Arrow*. Films may provide good points of departure for discussions of music and dance, historical perspectives, lifestyles, and so on.

## NOTE

1. *Canku Ota (Many Paths), An Online Newsletter Celebrating Native America* 6, September 7, 2002, www.turtletrack.org/Issues02/Co09072002/CO_09072002_Secola.htm.

## DISCOGRAPHY

In addition to the recordings referenced in the main body of this chapter and in individual lessons, the following recordings offer only a few of the possible resources available for use in the music classroom. Online catalogs for Canyon Records, Sounds of America Records, and other companies specializing in Native American music, as well as online sites with all music to be legally downloaded, should be browsed for extended listings and the latest releases. Some sites for downloads include:

Apple iTunes: http://apple.com/itunes/
Calabash: www.calabashmusic.com
C/Net Download: http://music.download.cnet.com
E-Music: http://emusic.com
Global Rhythm: http://globalrhythm.net/
Napster: www.napster.com/
Rhapsody: http://rhapsody.com
Smithsonian Folkways: www.folkways.si.edu/

*American Indian Sampler*, an iMix compiled by Kay Edwards, Miami University of Ohio. Individual songs may be downloaded from iTunes.

1. "Round Dance Song"/John Rainer Jr.
2. "Owl Dance"/Blackfoot Confederacy
3. "Medley: 4 Moccasin Games Songs—Ye'iitsoh Song"/Navajo Songs
4. "Moccasin Game Song"/A. Paul Ortega and Sharon Burch
5. "Dakota Love Song"/Robert Tree Cody
6. "Nana's Lullaby"/Mary Youngblood
7. "Lakota Lullaby"/Robert Tree Cody
8. "Oneida Iroquois"/Joanne Shenandoah
9. "Navajo"/Julia Begaye
10. "Navajo: Song of Happiness"/Native Americans
11. "Hopi Harvest Dance"/Ed Lee Natay
12. "Children's Dance"/Mary Youngblood
13. "Friendship Song"/Joanne Shenandoah
14. "We Are Here"/Sharon Burch
15. "Pascola Dance-Mamna Cillim" (Green Spinach/Yaqui Ritual and Festive Music/Musicians from Old Paschua Village, Sonora, Tucson, and Rio Yaqui)
16. "Deer Dance-Tosay Hwilit" (White Bird and Taciovakok/Yaqui Ritual and Festive Music)
17. "Daybreak Vision"/R. Carlos Nakai/*Canyon Trilogy*
18. "Daybreak Vision"/R. Carlos Nakai/*Inner Voices*
19. "The Indians Win"/Brent Michael Davids
20. "The Dance"/Robert Mirabal
21. "Christopher Columbus"/XIT
22. "Let's Save Our Mother Earth"/Robby Bee and the Boyz from the Rez
23. "Jingle Bells"/Southern Scratch
24. "War Dance Song"/Alvin Ahoy-Boy/Indian Chipmunks
25. "Old MacDonald Had a Farm"/Black Lodge Singers
26. "Sponge Bob Square Pants"/Black Lodge Singers

*Contemporary Native American Sampler*, an iMix compiled by Bryan Burton, West Chester University, contains samples of contemporary Native American music ranging from rock to jazz to hip-hop to country. Individual songs may be downloaded from iTunes.

1. "Christopher Columbus"/XIT/*Without Reservation*
2. "1492 Who Found Who"/Murray Porter/*1492 Who Found Who*
3. "Seven Generations"/Brule/*Star People*
4. "Let's Save Our Mother Earth"/Robby Bee and the Boyz from the Rez/*Reservation of Education*
5. "You Can Hear Them Dancing"/Joanne Shenandoah/*Once in a Red Moon*
6. "Frybread"/Native Roots/*Rain Us Love*
7. "Custer"/Mike Trailwalker Wilson/*Native Country*
8. "Going Home"/Ulali/*Heartbeat: Voices of First Nations Women*
9. "One Drop of Blood"/Cherokee National Children's Choir/*Voices of the Creator's Children*
10. "Two World Concerto"/R. Carlos Nakai/*Two World Concerto*
11. "Indians Win Again"/Brent Michael Davids/*Bright Circle*
12. "Up Where We Belong"/Buffy Saint Marie/*Up Where We Belong*
13. "The Dance"/Robert Mirabal/*Music from a Painted Cave*

## Anthologies

*The American Indian*. Robbie Robertson and the Red Road Ensemble. CDP 7243
*Anthology of North American Indian and Eskimo Music*. Smithsonian Folkways, FW04541.
*Creations Journey*. Smithsonian Folkways, SF 40410.
*Heartbeat: Voices of First Nation's Women*. Smithsonian Folkways, SF CD40415.
*Heartbeat 2: More Voices of First Nation's Women*. Smithsonian Folkways, SF CD40445.
*Under the Green Corn Moon*. Silver Wave Records, SD 916.
*Wood That Sings*. Smithsonian Folkways, SFW40472.

## Arctic

*The Eskimos of Hudson Bay and Alaska.* Smithsonian Folkways, FW4444
*Inuit Games and Songs.* Phillips, 6586036.
*The Inuit of the Arctic Circle.* Lyrachord, LLst 7379 and 7380.
*Inuit Throat and Harp Songs.* Canadian Music Heritage, MH 001.
*Songs of the Iglulik Inuit.* Berlin Museum Collection, CD 19.

## Basin and Plateau/California

ISHI: *The Last Yahi.* This was recorded from 1911 to 1914. Wild Sanctuary.
*Songs of Love, Luck, Animals, and Magic.* Nightwork, NW 297.
*Songs of the Paiute, Washoe, Ute, Bannock, Shoshone.* Library of Congress, LC 38.
*Starting Over (Yampaciki Singers).* Sounds of America Records, SOAR 155.
*Utes-War, Bear, and Sun Dance Songs.* Canyon Records, CR 6113.

## Contemporary

See figure 4.1 for a sampler of contemporary styles from rock and jazz to hip-hop, reggae, and country that may be downloaded from iTunes. Several contemporary selections may also be found on the *American Indian Sample iMix.* Other recordings that may be of use in the music classroom include:

*Bright Circle.* Brent Michael Davids. Download from www.apple.com/itunes (contemporary orchestral).
*Circle.* Performed and produced by Keith Secola. Akina Productions.
*Dreaming in Color.* Performed by Songcatcher. A&M Records, 31454-0247-2.
*Kokopelli's Café.* Performed by R. Carlos Nakai Quartet. Canyon Records, CR 7013.
*Makoce Wakan.* Performed by Red Thunder. Eagle Thunder Records, 3-7916-2-H1 c/o Koch Intertribal, 2 Tri-Harbor Court, Port Washington, NY 11050.
*Music from a Painted Cave.* Performed by Robert Mirabal and the Rare Tribal Mob.
*Native Americana.* Performed by Keith Secola. Akina Recordings.
*Old Time Chicken Scratch.* Performed by the Gu Achi Fiddlers. Canyon Records, CR 8092.
*Once in a Red Moon.* Performed by Joanne Shenandoah. Canyon Records, CR 548.
*Plight of the Redman.* Performed by Tom Bee and XIT. Sounds of America Records, SOAR 101-CD. Available from Sounds of America Records, PO Box 8207, Albuquerque, NM 87198.
*Southern Scratch*, Vol. 1. Canyon Records, CR 8093.
*Spirit Horses.* Performed by Nakai and DeMars. Canyon Records, CR 7014.
*Yazzie Girl.* Performed by Sharon Burch. Canyon Records, CR 534.

## Eastern Woodlands

*Earth Songs.* Allegany Singers. Self-produced.
*Free Spirit Micmac Songs.* Performed by Free Spirit. Sunshine Records Limited. SSCT 4093. Sunshine Records Limited, 275 Selkirk Ave., Winnipeg, Manitoba, R2W 2L5 Canada.
*Red Thundercloud.* Performed by the Catawba tribe. Hilljoy Records.
*Seneca Social Dance Music.* Folkways Ethnic. FE 4072.
*Songs and Dances of the Eastern Indians from Medicine Spring and Allegany.* New World Records. NW 337.
*Songs and Dances of the Great Lakes Indians.* Smithsonian Folkways. FW04003.
*Songs of the Seminole Indians of Florida.* Smithsonian Folkways. FW04383.
*We Will Sing!* Edadrenodo:nyo. Performed by Six Nations Women Singers. Sounds of America Records, SOAR 175.

## Native American Flute

*Buffalo Spirit.* Performed by Fernando Cellicion. Indian Sounds Recordings, IS 5062. Indian Sounds Recordings, PO Box 6038, Moore, OK 73153.
*Canyon Trilogy.* Performed by R. Carlos Nakai. Canyon Records, CR 610.
*Dreamcatcher.* Performed by Kevin Locke. Earth Beat Records, EB 2995.
*Dreams from the Grandfathers.* Performed by Robert Tree Cody. Canyon Records, CR 554.
*Songs of the American Indian Flute*, Vols. 1 and 2. Performed by John Ranier Jr. Red Willow Songs.
*Traditional and Contemporary Indian Flute.* Performed by Tom Ware. Indian Sounds Recordings, IS 5050. Indian Sounds Recording.

## Northern Plains

*Crow Grass Dance and Owl Dance.* Sound Chief. Indian House Records, SC 116.
*Intertribal Powwow Songs.* Performed by Kicking Women Singers. Canyon Records, CR 6178.
*Mandan-Hidatsa Songs.* Performed by the Mandaree Singers. Canyon Records, CR 6114.
*Plains Chippewa/Metis Music from Turtle Mountain.* Smithsonian Folkways, SF 40411.
*Rabbit Songs of the Lakota,* Vol. 5. Performed by Porcupine Singers. Canyon Records. CR 6191.

## Northwest Coast

*Chemiwci Singers.* Performed by the Chemiwci Indian School of Salem, OR. Canyon Records, CR 6121.
*Indian Music of the Pacific Northwest.* Folkways Ethnic, FE 4523.
*Songs of the Warm Springs Reservation.* Canyon Records, CR 6123.
*Stick Game Songs.* Performed by Joe Washington Lummi. Canyon Records, CR 6124.

## Southern Plains

*Hand Game of the Kiowa, Kiowa-Apache, and Comanche,* Vols. 1 and 2. Indian House Records, IH 2501 and IH 2502.
*Intertribal Songs of Oklahoma.* Performed by Southern Thunder. Indian House Records, IH 2081.
*Kiowa Gourd Dance,* Vol. 1. Indian House Records, IH 2503.
*Round Dance Songs with English Lyrics.* Performed by Ware/Moore. Indian Sounds Recordings, IS 1004.
*Songs of the Comanche, Cheyenne, Kiowa, Caddo, Wichita, Pawnee.* Library of Congress, LC 39.

## Southwest

*Hopi Social Dance Songs,* Vol. 2. Canyon Records, CR 6108.
*Music from Zuni Pueblo.* Performed by Chester Mahooty. Tribal Music International, TMI 008. Available from *Music of New Mexico: Native American Traditions.* Smithsonian Folkways, SF 40408.
*Navajo Social Dance Songs.* Performed by the Turtle Mountain Singers. Indian House Records, IH 1523.
*Round Dance Songs* or *Taos Pueblo.* Vol. 1. Indian House Records, IH 1001.
*Songs of the White Mountain Apache.* Canyon Records, CR 6165.
*When the Earth Was like New.* Performed by Chesley Goseyun Wilson. World Music Press.
*Yaquii Ritual and Festive* Music. Canyon Records, CR 6190.

Many of the above recordings are available from:

Akina Recordings. PO Box 1595, Tempe, AZ 85280
Canyon Records and Indian Arts, 4143 North 16th Street, Phoenix, AZ 85016; telephone: 602-266-4823
Eagle Thunder Records, c/o Koch Intertribal, 2 Tri-Harbor Court, Port Washington, NY 11050
Indian House Records, PO Box 472, Taos, NM 87571
Indian Sounds Recordings, PO Box 6038, Moore, OK 73153
Sounds of America Records, PO Box 8207, Albuquerque, NM 87110
Sunshine Records Limited, 275 Selkirk Ave., Winnipeg, Manitoba, R2W 2L5 Canada
Tribal Music International, 449 Juan Tomas, Tijeras, NM 87059

# FILMOGRAPHY

Most of the following DVDs are available from any major online service.

*American Indian Dance Theatre: Dances for the New Generations.* Available from PDR Productions, 219 East 44th Street, New York, NY 10017. This video contains songs and dances from the northwest coast, New England, New York, Oklahoma, and the Great Plains. Not only does this video show performances by the American Indian Dance Theatre, but it also shows members of the troupe learning the dances from tribal leaders around the country.
*American Indian Dance Theatre: Finding the Circle.* Available through PDR Productions, 219 East 44th Street, New York, NY 10017. This is a performance by the American Indian Dance Theatre for the Great Performances public television special. Narration provides the cultural background for each dance. Many tribes are represented from across the United States, and the video shows powwows and intertribal songs and dances.

*Entering the Circle*. Available from American Orff-Schulwerk Association, PO Box 391089, Cleveland, OH 44139. This is a videotape of a session presented at the 1994 AOSA Conference by J. Bryan Burton. This video contains demonstrations of several dances, an overview of cultural contexts, and a display of representative instruments.

*Into the Circle*: An *Introduction into Oklahoma Pow-wows and Celebrations*. Available from Canyon Records, 4143 North 16th Street, Phoenix, AZ 85016. This video describes and gives background information on the powwow traditions in Oklahoma. A number of dances are shown in actual performance situations.

*Music from a Painted Cave*. Robert Mirabal and the Rare Tribal Mob. Red Feather Studio. Wide-ranging performance by Robert Mirabal including clips showing traditional life in contemporary Taos Pueblo.

*The Native Americans*. Available from Turner Home Entertainment, One CNN Center, Atlanta, GA 30303. This well-documented and well-produced series is based on the book of the same name. Tribal elders, musicians, and historians provide insights and performances including stories, songs, and dances. There are six volumes in this series; each focuses on a specific region: 3214 *The Nations of the Northeast*; 3215 *The Tribal People of the Northwest*; 3216 *Tribes of the Southeast*; 3217 *The Natives of the Southwest*; 3218 *The People of the Great Plains, Part One*; and 3219 *The People of the Great Plains, Part Two*.

*Powwow Trail* is a series of DVDs from Arbor Records, Winnipeg, Canada, with each video focusing upon a particular aspect of the intertribal powwow. Some of the volumes available include:

*Pow Wow Trail*, Vol. 1: "The Drum"
*Pow Wow Trail*, Vol. 2: "The Songs"
*Pow Wow Trail*, Vol. 3: "The Dances "
*Pow Wow Trail*, Vol. 4: "The Grand Entry"
*Pow Wow Trail*, Vol. 5: "Grass Dance and Men's Traditional"
*Pow Wow Trail*, Vol. 6: "The Fancy Dance"
*Pow Wow Trail*, Vol. 7: "Pow Wow Rock"
*Pow Wow Trail*, Vol. 8: "Women"
*Pow Wow Trail*, Vol. 9: "The Grand Exhibition"
*Pow Wow Trail*, Vol. 10: "The White Man's Indian"

*Seasons: A Celebration of Native American, Polynesian, and Latin American Music and Dance*. Brigham Young University.

*Songs of Indian Territory: Native American Musical Traditions of Oklahoma*. Available from Canyon Records, 4143 North 16th Street, Phoenix, AZ. Songs and dances are described and shown on film. A number of tribes from Oklahoma are portrayed.

*Thunder in the Dells*. Produced for the Wisconsin Winnebago people showing their history and culture. Several songs and dances are presented as part of the narrative. Available from Ootek Productions, SI2229 Round River Trail, Spring Green, WI 53588.

*Trudell*. Passion River Studio. Featuring Native American political activist and musician John Trudell.

*Up Where We Belong*. Image Entertainment. Part documentary, part performance, part interview featuring Buffy Saint Marie, composer of the only Native American song to receive an Oscar for Best Song in a Motion Picture.

*XIT without Reservation*. SOAR (Sound of America Records). XIT'S thirtieth anniversary concert at Mystic River Casino.

# BIBLIOGRAPHY

Ballard, Louis W. *American Indian Music for the Classroom*. Santa Fe, N.M.: New Southwest Music Publications, 2004.

Bigelow, B., and B. Peterson. *Rethinking Columbus: The Next 500 years*. Milwaukee, Wis.: Rethinking Schools, 1998.

Burton, J. Bryan. *Moving within the Circle: Contemporary Native American Music and Dance*. 2nd ed. Danbury, Conn.: World Music Press, 2008.

———. "Native American Music." In *Encyclopedia of the Great Plains*, edited by David J. Wishart. Lincoln: University of Nebraska Press, 2007.

———. *Voices of the Wind: Native American Flute Songs*. Danbury, Conn.: World Music Press, 1998.

Burton, J. Bryan, Chesley Wilson, and Ruth Wilson. *When the Earth Was Like New: Western Apache Stories and Songs*. Danbury, Conn.: World Music Press, 1994.

Curtis, Natalie. *The Indians' Book*. New York: Dover Publications, 1994.

Deloria, Philip. *Indians in Unexpected Places*. Lawrence: University Press of Kansas, 2004.

Deloria, Philip, and Neal Salisbury, eds. *A Companion to American Indian History*. Oxford: Blackwell, 2004.

Densmore, Frances: multiple texts, each exploring the music and culture of a specific tribe/nation or region including *Chippewa Music I and II*; *Teton Sioux Music and Culture*; *Seminole Music*; *Music of Acoma, Isleta, Cochiti, and Zuni Pueblos*; *Yuman and Yaqui Music*; *Papago Music*; and many, many others. Browse through an online bookstore for a more complete listing.

Diamond, Beverley. *Native American Music in Eastern North America*. New York: Oxford University Press, 2008.

Diamond, Beverley, et al. *Visions of Sound: Musical Instruments of First Nations Communities in Northeastern America*. Chicago: University of Chicago Press, 1994.

Ellis, Clyde. *A Dancing People: Powwow Culture on the Southern Plains*. Lawrence: University Press of Kansas, 2003.

Hirschfelder, A., P. Molin, and Y. Wakim. *American Indian Stereotypes in the World of Children*. London: Scarecrow Press, 1999.

Heth, Charlotte, ed. *Native American Dance: Ceremonies and Social Traditions*. Washington, DC: Smithsonian Books, 1992.

Howard, James H., and Victoria Levine. *Choctaw Music and Dance*. Norman: University of Oklahoma Press, 1990.

Jones, G., and S. Moomaw. "Lessons from Turtle Island: Native American Curriculum." In *Early Childhood Classrooms*. St. Paul, Minn.: Redleaf Press, 2002.

Keeling, Richard. *North American Indian Music: A Guide to Published Sources and Selected Recordings*. New York: Garland Publishing, 1997.

Laubin, Reginald, and Gladys Lauin. *Indian Dances of North America*. Norman: University of Oklahoma Press, 1977.

McAllester, David P. "North American Native Music." In *Music of Many Cultures*, edited by Elizabeth May. New York: Schirmer Books, 1992.

McAllester, David P., and David Schupman. "Teaching the Music of the American Indian." In *Teaching Music with a Multicultural Approach*, edited by William Anderson. Reston, Va.: MENC, 1991.

Nakai, R. Carlos, James DeMars, Ken Light, and David P. McAllester. *The Art of the Native American Flute*. Phoenix: Canyon Records, 1996.

Pisani, Michael V. *Imagining Native America in Music*. New Haven, Conn.: Yale University Press, 2005.

Rodriquez, Sylvia. *The Matachines Dance: Ritual and Interethnic Relations in the Upper Rio Grande Valley*. Albuquerque: University of New Mexico Press, 1996.

Samuels, David. *Putting a Song on Top of It: Expression and Identity on the San Carlos Apache Reservation*. Tucson: Arizona University Press, 2006.

Seale, D., and B. Slapin. *A Broken Flute: The Native Experience in Books for Children*. Walnut Creek, Calif.: Altamira Press, 2005.

———. *Through Indian Eyes: The Native Experience in Books for Children*. Los Angeles: University of California Los Angeles American Indian Studies Center Publications, 1998.

Sweet, Jill. *Dances of Tewa Indians: Expressions of New Life*. Rev ed. Santa Fe, N.M.: School of American Research Press, 2004.

Vander, Judith. *Songprints: The Music Experience of Five Shoshone Women*. Urbana: University of Illinois Press, 1988.

## Internet Resources

www.goodminds.com
www.fourdirectionsteachings.com
www.nativedance.ca
www.nativedrums.ca
www.nativeradio.com
www.nativeculture.com
www.native-languages.org
www.ohwejagehka.com
www.powwow.com
www.nativeamericanmusicawards.com
For more information regarding selected Nations, the following websites may prove useful:

Alabama-Coushatta: www.alabama-coushatta.com
Apache: www.carizona.com/super/attractions/san_carlos.htm
Cherokee: www.cherokee.org
Choctaw: www.choctawnation.com
Haliwa-Saponi: www.ncsu.edu/stud_orgs/native_american/nctribes_orgs/haliwa.htm
Hidatsa: www.mhanation.com
Kiowa: www.ohwy.com/ok/k/kiowamuse.com
Lakota: www.olc.com (site for Oglala Lakota College)
Navajo: www.navajo.org
Tigua: www.texasindians.com/tigua.htm
Yaqui: www.pascuayaqui-nsn.gov
Zuni: www.ashiwi.org/list.html

## Native Performers

Many Native performers maintain websites either as individuals or through recording companies. A few sites are listed below. If your favorite performer is not listed, trying a search for the artist's name.

Chesley Goseyun Wilson: www.elearn.arizona.edu/msw/apache/chesley/aboutchesley.html
Fernando Cellicion: www.nativestars.com/fernando

Joanne Shenandoah: www.joanneshenandoah.com
Kevin Locke: www.kevinlocke.com
R. Carlos Nakai: www.canyonrecords.com/artnakai.htm or www.nakaiquartet.com
Robert Mirabal: www.mirabal.com
Robert Tree Cody: www.treecody.com
Sharon Burch: www.canyonrecords.com/artburch.htm
Tom Bee: www.soundofamerica.com
Walela (Rita Coolidge and family): www.walela.com

## Selected Native-Owned Recording Companies

Canyon Records: www.canyonrecords.com
Eagle Thunder Records: www.eaglethunder.com
Indian House Recordings: www.indianhouse.com
Indian Sounds Recordings: www.indiansounds.tripod.com
Sound of America Recordings (SOAR): www.soundofamerica.com

## Selected Sources for Native American Instruments and Crafts

Amon Olorin Flutes: www.aoflutes.com
Flutes by Coyote Oldman: www.coyoteoldman.com
Indian Pueblo Cultural Center: www.indianpueblo.org
Lakota Crafts: www.lakotafund.org
Taos Drums: www.taosdrums.com

# 5

## Music of Oceania and the Pacific

*Ann Clements, Peter Dunbar-Hall, and Sarah Watts*

The Pacific Ocean, the world's largest and deepest ocean covering about one-third of the earth's surface, is home to the continent Australia and 25,000 to 30,000 coral atolls and volcanic islands grouped into Melanesia, Micronesia, and Polynesia.[1] Tourism and the media provide images of palm trees, sandy beaches, and a laid-back lifestyle, but little is conveyed of the complexities of cultural groups who live there. The Pacific islands and Australia are comprised of some of the planet's oldest and most complicated cultural groups. Pacific peoples vary in ethnicity, language, and religion. While some cultural groupings can trace their genealogy to common ancestry, the region has a long history of migration that has allowed for cultures to develop slowly over time. This long history of culture has made Oceania and the Pacific a multidimensional geographic area of many peoples and many musics.

### MAPPING PACIFIC ISLAND TRAVELS

As the Pacific is filled with islands, it follows that island inhabitants employed sea travel to arrive at their various island homes. While there are still many unknowns about when people arrived and the navigation passages they used to find these islands, it is possible to estimate their travel and suggest a common ancestry among some culture groups. Ancient Pacific Islanders' voyages were motivated for multiple reasons including war, trade, colonization, curiosity, and the ongoing search for new resources. Navigation techniques consisted of complex oceanic knowledge that was passed by oral tradition from navigator to apprentice. This knowledge included the motion of specific stars and astral alignment, weather patterns, times of travel wildlife species and bird migration (which congregate at particular positions), directions of swells on the ocean, the colors of the sea and sky, and cloud clustering. To this day there remains great pride among Pacific peoples in their history of migration and the high technical skills their ancestors maintained in navigating the open ocean.

While we often refer to the vessels used for travel around the Pacific as "canoes" it is important to realize that this term is somewhat misleading. While vessels ranged in size from small to large, some of the larger vessels were thirty yards in length and could accommodate hundreds of men and their materials. These crafts, either double canoes or single canoes with outriggers, carried one or more masts and sails of woven materials. James Cook and contemporary observers estimated that Pacific canoes were capable of greater speeds than their own ships, probably 90 to 150 miles per day, so that trips of 3,000 miles or more could be comfortably achieved with available provisions. The theme of canoe travel is very much a constant in Pacific island music, art, and folklore.

It has been estimated that people first reached the Pacific islands 50,000 years ago, arriving in New Guinea from Southeast Asia via Indonesia. These first people now known as Papuans may share ancestry with Australia's first Aborigines. Moving slowly to the east, the Papuans were stopped in the northern Solomon Islands about 25,000 years ago due to the great navigational distance between the Solomon Islands and the islands further to the east. Around the same time period, another group of people collectively called the Austronesians moved into this area from the west and mingled with the Papuans forming the highly diverse group we currently call the Melanesians.

New Guinea and the Solomon Islands are presumed to have been the only inhibited islands in the South Pacific for thousands of years. The wider seas between the Solomons and Vanuatu were finally crossed in about 1500 BCE. The

Lapta people, who were Austronesian peoples, gathered the skills needed to cross the open seas and landed in New Caledonia. Heading further east, they began to inhabit Fiji, Tonga, and Samoa, where they developed the cultures we commonly refer to as Polynesian. At some time around 200 BCE they crossed over the longer ocean passages to the east including the Society and Marquises island groups (French Polynesia), and onward to Rarotonga and the South Cook Islands, Rapa Nui (Easter Islands) in CE 300, North to Hawaii around CE 400 and southwest past Rarontonga to Aotearoa (New Zealand) in CE 800–900.

## PACIFIC CULTURES AND CUSTOMS

The peoples and cultures of this region are just as diverse as the 64.9 million square mile ocean that surrounds them. Many of the early musics of the Pacific consisted mainly of vocal chant-like singing with little to no harmonic structure and some use of membranophones, aerophones, and simple idiophones. The use of traditional instrumentation is extreme with panpipes playing a large role in the Solomon Islands to body percussion playing large roles in Aotearoa (New Zealand) and Samoan Islands. In most areas of the Pacific there was no written language prior to colonization and music served a tremendous role in maintaining cultural knowledge, history, and genealogy, and played a significant role in both secular and religious life. In modern Pacific life, musical preferences are similar to many other areas of the world with traditional musics residing alongside more popular styles, and, in many cases, Pacific peoples have found innovative ways in which to incorporate the two together.

Within most musics of the Pacific, the lyrics of songs are far more important than the melodic accompaniment, which sometimes has been purposefully changed in modern times to Western pop music structures. Musical elements and dance are traditionally viewed as accompaniment to the lyrics, which are the primary focus, with the music and dance serving to embellish, illustrate, and decorate the words. Due to the heavy influence of modern Western musical practices, a traditional melody is considered no more Polynesian than the same song sung to a modern "imported" melody.

Song and dance are integral parts of the same cultural elements throughout Polynesia. In action songs (songs that have accompanying dance that bring the lyrical material into physical space), dance is used to illustrate the lyrics by moving the hands or arms and some dances, such as the *mā'ulu'ulu* from Samoa, are performed while seated. Traditionally, dance moves do not illustrate the song's narrative, but rather draw attention to specific words and themes; in modern times, however, dances are more often explicitly narrative in their focus. There are also traditional dances performed without lyrics, to the accompaniment of percussive music.

### Hawaiian

Hawaiian music is a rich plethora of traditional and modern styles ranging from native Hawaiian chants to slack-key and steel guitar and ukulele styles to rock and hip-hop. Traditional Hawaiian folk music remains a major part of the state's traditional heritage. Their music is largely religious in nature and contains both chant and dance musics. Hawaiian folk music includes several varieties of chanting (*mele*) and music meant for highly ritualized dance (*hula*). Traditional Hawaiian music and dance was functional, used to express praise, communicate genealogy and mythology, and accompany games, festivals, and other secular events.

The Hawaiian language has no word that translates precisely as music, instead a diverse vocabulary exists to describe rhythms, instruments, styles, and elements of voice production. Hawaiian music may appear simple in melody and rhythm compared to some of its Pacific neighbors, but it is rich in its poetic nature and the subtlety of it vocal lines. There are primarily two forms of chanting: *mele oli* and *mele hula*. Mele oli is often enjoyed for its natural a cappella sonic beauty and it is common to hear the mele hula as an accompaniment for dance (hula). The chanters are known as *haku mele* and are highly trained composers and performers. Some chants are written to express specific emotions, others are for prayer, and some are recitations of genealogy or historical records related to significant cultural events. Mele is often accompanied by the *ipu heke*, which is a double-sided gourd that is played both by striking the side of the instrument and by hitting the instrument to the floor to achieve a deeper bass sound.

Hawaiians are known throughout the world for the beauty, gracefulness, and deep poetic nature of their traditional dance: hula. The hula is traditionally accompanied by singing and some instrumentation. The purpose of the hula is to dramatize or comment on the mele that is being performed. There are typically two styles of hula, these being called *kahiko* and *'auana*. Kahiko, or ancient hula, is accompanied by chant and traditional instruments. 'Auana, which is a form of hula that has evolved under Western influence in the nineteenth and twentieth centuries, is accompanied by instruments such as the guitar, ukulele, and bass. Hula is taught in schools called *halau*. The teacher of hula is known as the *kumu hula*, where *kumu* means source of knowledge. Hula dancing is a complex art form, and there are many hand motions used to signify aspects of nature, such as the basic hula and coconut tree motions, or the basic leg steps, such as the *Kaholo, Ka'o, Hela, Uwehe,* and *Ami*.

## Maori

While Maori are considered part of Polynesia, their relative isolation in nautical distance from other Polynesian cultural groups has resulted in a distinctive musical tradition. They are probably best known around the world as performers of the *Haka* (an aggressive posture dance). The national rugby team, the All Blacks, perform this dance prior to the start of every game. Of equal merit and reputation is the rich and beautiful modern musical tradition of harmonic singing that is unique in its orientation and presentation. It is not uncommon for Maori ensembles to perform in six- to eight-part vocal harmonies. Prior to colonization Maori had no written language and it was through the arts that knowledge and tradition were passed from one generation to the next. Language (*te reo*) plays a key role in the singing of recitatives and song and even in modern times music remains a primary source of language and cultural maintenance.

Maori traditional music can be divided into two categories: recitatives and songs. Recitatives include: *powhiri* (a welcome ceremony recited by men and women), *haka taparahi* (a dance without weapons), *haka peruperu* (with weapons), *karakia* (incantations and spells), and *paatere* (reactions to gossip). Songs include: *poi* (songs accompanied by a dance in which women hit their body rhythmically with yarn, flax, or cotton balls attached to a string), *oriori* (songs composed to teach children of high rank their special descent and history), *pao* (improvised songs of local interest), *waiata aroha* (love songs), *waiata whaiaaipo* (laments), and *waiata tahit* (chants or song poetry often determined by a lyrical theme and accompanied by traditional instruments such as the *koauau* [rotund flute], *putorino* [small flute], *nguru* [nose flute], and *pututara* [conch shell]).

While all of these traditional styles play a large role in Maori culture, Maori people are also becoming well known for their significant contributions to popular music, specifically pop, rap, and hip-hop. As is common among postcolonial nations around the world, the influence of popular styles on traditional musics is tremendous. New Zealand is brimming with Maori, Pacifica, and world music sounds, and modern Maori music is often a hybrid cross between tradition and modernity. Since the 1970s there has been a cultural resurgence among the Maori people, bringing a new source of pride to their heritage. One of the main results has been the creation of new Maori sounds and musics. Regional, tribal, school, and community groups have created many new performance-based cultural opportunities to revive, and in some ways reinvent, what it means to be Maori and express *mana* (Maori spirit). There is mixed opinion on what constitutes "real Maori music," but it is sufficient to say that Maori culture expressed through music is vibrant and alive throughout Aotearoa (New Zealand).

## Samoan

Perhaps more than any other Polynesian culture, Samoans have maintained their traditional way of life and still closely follow their social hierarchies, customs, and courtesies. The Samoan Islands are divided into two political regions of Samoa (formally Western Samoa) and American Samoa. Samoa has a population of 165,000, the vast majority of whom live in or around the island of 'Upolu. American Samoa has a population of approximately 63,500 people, most of whom live on the main island Tutuila. The influence of two different colonial powers in the twentieth century has resulted in some distinct differences between these two groups. New Zealand's connection to Samoa and its wider British associations profoundly influenced development and education and opened up a diasporic pathway that flowed southward. American Samoa has shown little outwardly resistance to the military presence, as the U.S. government is a heavy employer in this island nation.

Musical expressions of many types find their home in Samoan culture and include instrumental and vocal music, as well as movement and dance. Samoan musical instruments are many and vary in form and function. Music and dance are accompanied by the *fala*, a rolled mat beaten with two light sticks to accompany group song, and the pate or slit drum introduced from Rarotonga in the nineteenth century. Body percussion in the form of hand clapping may be found in choral music settings as well as in various Samoan dances.

The spread of Christianity has resulted in the disappearance of some dances, making room for the dominant genre of *siva*, which is now performed at both formal and informal events. Siva may be accompanied by a wide range of singing and instrumentation from electric bands to a cappella choir and can be performed individually and improvised within a recognized range of hand, head, and feet movements. The mā'ulu'ulu dance was created at the end of the nineteenth century and is today one of the most dynamic displays of synchronized group performance, involving a mixture of sitting, kneeling, and standing and sometimes a division of dancers into separate sets of action sequences, followed by choreographed movements performed by a seated group moving to the steady beat of a tin drum or pate. The famous Samoan fire dance, or *'ailao*, did not develop until in the mid-twentieth century and quickly spread throughout Polynesia, now serving as a popular marker of tourism in Pacific culture. With regard to vocal music, songs are often composed for special occasions or to commemorate an important event. Song text is critical to performance and both the music and dance performed by village groups are strong statements of identity. The taualuga often completes a performance and demonstrates the interrelations of "chiefs" and "orators" within Samoan culture.

## INDIGENOUS PEOPLES OF AUSTRALIA

Indigenous Australians are the descendants of the first known inhabitants of the Australian continent and its surrounding islands. They are considered to have inhabited the Australian mainland and its associated islands for at least 50,000 years. Among the earliest inhabitants of the Oceania region, it is generally accepted that Indigenous Australians entered Australia from the Indo-Malaysian mainland via New Guinea, taking advantage of the land bridges that stretched most of the way through Asia. The term Indigenous Australians encompasses many different communities and societies, and these are further divided into local communities with unique cultures and separate languages. The term incorporates both Torres Strait Islanders and Aboriginal people, who together comprise approximately 2.4 percent of Australia's modern society. While there is no clear or accepted origin of Indigenous Australians, it is commonly believed that they migrated to Australia through Southeast Asia and that they are not demonstrably related to any known Asian or Polynesian peoples. There is, however, evidence of genetic and linguistic interchange between Australians in the far north and the Austronesian peoples of modern-day New Guinea and the islands of Indonesia. Archaeological finds estimate their arrival in Australia 3,400 years ago. While there were originally over 250 languages spoken by the Australians, only approximately 70 of these remain in use today, and all but 20 of those in use are considered to be endangered.

### Indigenous Australian Cultures and Customs

Music is central to the many cultures of Indigenous Australians. Music in these cultures represents a point of contact to the knowledge one must have about one's culture and their place within it, and about their connection with the natural and supernatural realms. From a young age, children are encouraged to move, dance, and sing to everyday tasks. As they mature they are entrusted with songs, which encapsulate deeply meaningful lessons about totemic plants and animals of their clan, and the history and mythology of the group. In these cultures such songs belong to their personal lineage and have specific melodic formulas and modes that distinguish one group from another. As they age, children's knowledge of these songs grows and this knowledge is often considered a source of personal strength for them, their families, and communities.

Although there are variations in the customs and skills of the different Aboriginal communities across the vast continent of Australia, they all live in equally close contact with the natural environment. Religious beliefs (sometimes referred to by non-Aboriginal people as the Dreamtime) encouraged intimate involvement with the landscape, whether a person's home was on the lush coastal plains or in the harsh interior. Aboriginal people knew what to eat, how to prepare it, where and when to find it and, most importantly, how to protect their resources for the future. What the elders knew about survival, they passed on by example, legend, and ritual through story, painting, song, and dance. Along with this, there were songs for different occasions—hunting songs, funeral songs, gossip songs, and songs of ancestors, landscapes, animals, seasons, history, myths, and legends.

Traditional songs are often sung as a series, comprised of many short independent verses. Each verse tells about a particular event, place, or emotion associated with a particular ancestor. A full ceremonial performance may include the portrayal of relevant events in the performance of dances accompanied by the singing of appropriate verses. Often dancers are decorated with body painting that relates to the story being acted out. In songs associated with any one totemic emblem there will be one melodic form throughout. This means, in the case of very long phrases of songs and stories, where the ancestor is reputed to have crossed thousands of miles of territory, the characteristic melodic line will be found across multiple cultural groupings with different languages and musical techniques. This movement of song allows flexibility in musical expression that tends to change from one community to another.

The traditional instrumentation of Indigenous Australian consists mainly of idiophones, membranophones, and aerophones. While Indigenous Australians are frequently associated with the didgeridoo (a hollowed-out tree branch or trunk that is blown through to create a drone-like sound) they are also well known for their use of the bullroarer (a piece of wood, bone, or rock tied to the end of a long string and spun overhead to create a whirling sound), clapsticks (two pieces of wood that are clapped together lengthwise), and the gumleaf (a Eucalyptus leaf held closely to the lips and blown through).

Modern Aboriginal musics are often a collaboration of new sounds and old traditions. Similar to other cultures of the Pacific, Indigenous Australians are redefining what their cultures are and mean in modern times and much of this is happening through musical creation and performance. Since the early 1980s, Aboriginal musicians have been navigating difficult waters between pure traditions, which can be thought of as the essential, and pure contemporary, which is often thought of as assimilation. This has resulted in multiple new musics including rock, reggae, country, hip-hop, and fusion often with lyrics based of social, cultural, and economic issues. It is not uncommon for traditional instruments and some traditional songs to be incorporated into these more modern musics.

## LESSON 1: INDIGENOUS AUSTRALIAN COMPOSING WITH THE DIDGERIDOO (GRADES 5–12)

**National Standards**

- Singing alone, and with others, a varied repertoire of music
- Performing on instruments, alone and with others, a varied repertoire of music
- Composing and arranging music within specified guidelines
- Listening to, analyzing, and describing music
- Evaluating music and music performances
- Understanding music in relation to history and culture

**Objectives**

Students will:

1. sing a song in the style of traditional Australian Aboriginal music;
2. create the text of a song;
3. add a drone to the song rhythm accompaniment on suitable instruments.

**Materials**

1. Map of Australia
2. Clapsticks, claves, or suitable pieces of wood
3. Instruments to provide drones
4. Recording from Smithsonian Folkways, "Bunggridj-bunggridj: Wangga Songs" by Alan Maralung with Peter Manaberu (SFW40430)—any tracks from this recording may be used throughout the lesson. (See www.folkways.si.edu.)

**Procedures**

1. View the map of Australia and provide important background information to students.
   a. Australian Aborigines live across Australia in a range of lifestyles. Some live and work in cities, others maintain lives close to the land. In parts of Australia songs from the past are still performed. In some areas solo singing is accompanied by didgeridoo and clapsticks.
   b. Additional information on Australian Aborigines can be found at: www.aboriginalaustralia.com/ or www.aboriginalart.com.au/ or www.indigenousaustralia.frogandtoad.com.au/.
2. Listen to tracks from "Bunggridj-bunggridj: Wangga Songs" by Alan Maralung, identifying how voice, didgeridoo, and clapsticks combine in performance of Aboriginal song.
3. Lead students through a discussion of aboriginal musical elements.
   a. In traditional Australian Aboriginal songs, melodies are often a series of repetitions of a descending phrase. Often the last repetition is followed by a series of repeated notes on the last pitch of the song. The following figure 5.1 shows this:

**Figure 5.1 Series of repeated notes**

This lesson was contributed by Peter Dunbar-Hall.

b. Words often refer to animal figures, aspects of landscape, an event (both from the past and more current times), or use vocables (syllables with no obvious meaning such as *na-na-na* or *jat-jat-jat*). A nasal sound quality is often used so that the sound can be heard well outdoors.

4. Sing the melody above adding words and vocables. Decide for yourself how many times you think the melody should be sung—many Aboriginal songs are quite short, so even a small number of repetitions will be acceptable. Some songs are sung as solos, while others are sung by groups of people. Decide how you will use solo singing and group singing to perform your song.

5. Lead students through a discussion of the didgeridoo (download a picture from www.images.google.com and project it on a screen for the class to see).

a. In parts of Australia the didgeridoo provides a drone accompaniment to Aboriginal songs. A didgeridoo is made from the hollow branch or trunk of a tree. The hollowing is done by termites eating away the wood inside a branch or trunk. Once cleaned out, a didgeridoo is cut until it produces the pitch a player wants. There is no uniformity of size, bore, or pitch. Wax or resin is spread around the end to be blown. Often a player decorates a didgeridoo with designs that reflect personal or group identity. Modern didgeridoos are made from plastic, cardboard, or even used car parts (such as exhaust pipes). You could experiment with different types of tubing to make your own didgeridoo-type instrument. A didgeridoo is blown the same way a trombone or tuba is blown—by buzzing the lips into the instrument. Pulsing (by moving the muscles of the diaphragm) can be used; imitating animal calls into the instrument is also a popular effect. Many didgeridoo players use circular breathing so that the sound they make is continuous until a piece of music ends. Listen to how the didgeridoois used on "Binggridj-bunggridj: Wangga Songs" by Alan Maralung. The pitch of the drone need not be related to that of the song—although this might occur coincidentally.

6. Have students add a drone to their previously created arrangement and repeat their performance. The drone can be done on any suitable instrument or can be hummed or sung.

7. Once the students can perform the song with drone accompaniment, add a rhythm part on clapsticks (claves or even pieces of branches can be used—for different sounds you can use a fork or spoon struck on a large can or box—while clapsticks or claves will give a sound similar to that heard on recordings, other sound sources are also acceptable). Usually the stick accompaniment to a song accentuates the pulse of the music. Sometimes rapid beating is used to indicate the end of a section of a song or of the song itself.

## Assessment

1. Students may demonstrate their understanding of the material through:

- recreation of the correct musical style;
- construction of appropriate topic of text; and
- creation of drone and appropriate stick accompaniment.

### LESSON 2: ROCK DIDGERIDOO (GRADES 5–12)

**National Standards**

- Singing alone, and with others, a varied repertoire of music
- Performing on instruments, alone and with others, a varied repertoire of music
- Composing and arranging music within specified guidelines
- Listening to, analyzing and describing music
- Evaluating music and music performances
- Understanding music in relation to history and culture

**Objectives**

Students will:

1. arrange the song from the previous lesson as a song in a popular music style;
2. incorporate musical aspects of the song into popular music sound styles;
3. perform the arranged song;
4. notate parts of the song.

**Materials**

1. Instruments for class use—rock drum kit, guitars, keyboards, clapsticks. If these instruments are not available, tunable drums, electronic music programs, or keyboards can be used to create meter and harmonic structures. There is also the option of having students use vocal sounds such as "beat boxing" for the rhythm and then singing repetitive ostinatos for a harmonic progression.
2. Recording "Dhayka Guyulinymirr" (track 7) from the album *Various—in Aboriginal* (2004). (See www.amazon .com/gp/product/B000QKNAG0/ref=dm_dp_adp?ie=UTF8&qid=1209097746&sr=103-1. This link takes the reader directly to the recording on Amazon.com. The track can be purchased immediately online independent of purchasing the entire album.)

**Procedures**

1. Lead students through a discussion of contemporary Australian Aboriginal music.
   a. Contemporary Australian Aboriginal musicians often arrange songs with didgeridoo and clapstick accompaniment as rock songs, or incorporate these songs into rock songs as sections of rock song structures.
   b. Often these new songs are used to discuss political issues, such as government treatment of indigenous people or loss of land. Sometimes such songs refer to indigenous people from other parts of the world to demonstrate similarity in living conditions. These songs also use Aboriginal languages to remind that Australian Aborigines have their own languages, many of which are dying out (the album *In Aboriginal* is made up of songs sung in a number of Aboriginal languages).
2. Listen to the track "Dhayka Guyulinymirr" (track 7) on the album *Various—in Aboriginal* for an example of didgeridoo played as an instrumental member of a rock ensemble.
3. Lead students through the creation of a rock arrangement of their previously created song from lesson 1 of this chapter. To create a rock song from the song they created in the previous lesson, students will need to decide what style of popular music to use. Reggae and country and western are popular with many Aboriginal musicians, as well as hip-hop and rap. Items students will need to create a new arrangement include:
   a. A written copy of the lyrics of the song
   b. Newly created rhythmical patterns to be played on drum kit, electronic music program, keyboard, or beat box
   c. Newly created chord patterns with optional bass line to be played or sung
   d. A format for the new arrangement, which may require the creation of new selections to be added to the original song
   e. Creative ways for the didgeridoo and clapsticks parts to be incorporated

---

This lesson was contributed by Peter Dunbar-Hall.

4. When these decisions have been made, guide students to perform their song. To assist in remembering it students may choose to notate the chord progression (letters can be used to represent the names of chords) and the rhythm parts.

5. Record the students' arrangement and play it back for the class. Ask students to draw conclusions about how their two arrangements are similar and different.

**Assessment**

1. Students may demonstrate their understanding of the material through:

   • demonstration of appropriate use of chosen musical style;
   • authentic and appropriate use of instrumentation;
   • appropriate integration of Aboriginal aspects; and
   • creation of correct and suitable notation.

## LESSON 3: MAORI WAIATA A RINGA (GRADES 7–12)

### National Standards

- Singing, alone and with others, a varied repertoire of music
- Composing and arranging music within specified guidelines
- Listening to, analyzing, and describing music
- Understanding music in relation to history and culture

### Objectives

Students will:

1. identify attributes of the Waiata a Ringa, after listening to "Aio" and "AEIOU";
2. sing a simplified version of "AEIOU";
3. dance to "AEIOU."

### Materials

1. Recordings

   - Recording "Aio" (Maori) from *Te Matarae Orehu: Maori Arts Festivals Winners "Live"* (track 5) available online from www .amazon.com/Maori-Arts-FestivalsWinners/dp/B000QR0OJY/ref=dm_ap_alb1?ie=UTF8&qid=1209427778&sr =1-127. (This link takes the reader directly to the recording online. The track can be purchased immediately, independent of purchasing the entire album.)

**Figure 5.2 AEIOU**

---

This lesson was contributed by Ann Clements.

- "AEIOU" (Maori) performed by Kahurangi from *Kahurangi: Music of the New Zealand Maori*, Smithsonian Folkways, FW04433 (www.folkways.si.edu.)

2. Guitar (optional)
3. Room for movement

**Procedures**

1. View the map of Aotearoa (New Zealand) and provide important background information to students. Aotearoa (Island of the Long White Cloud) is a grouping of three islands in the South Pacific Ocean in a region known as "Oceania." The main languages spoken are English and Maori. Maori are the indigenous peoples of New Zealand and make up approximately 15 percent of the total population. The center of traditional Maori life is the marae (meeting house). When you are welcomed on a marae you will be taken through a formal powhiri (welcoming) ceremony.

   a. Maps and other information can be found at https://www.cia.gov/library/publications/the-world-factbook/geos/nz.html or www.maori.org.nz/.
   b. Students can experience an interactive powhiri welcoming ceremony at www.holidays-in-newzealand.com/maori-powhri.html.

2. Have students listen to "Aio."
3. Lead a discussion with the students about their listening experience.

   a. Example questions: How would you describe this style of singing? Does it remind you of any styles of music or musical cultures you have heard before? What do feel this song is about?
   b. Possible answers include: This song is modern—it contains instrumentation (guitar), and there are specifically designated vocal harmonies. This song is intended for dancing and is a waiata a ringa (song with hands). The dancers portray the text with fluid movement of their bodies.
   c. A video of a waiata a ringa can be viewed at www.maori.org.nz/waiata/default.asp?pid=sp93&parent=84.

4. Have students listen to "AEIOU."
5. Lead a discussion about their listening experience.

   a. Example questions: How does this song differ from the previous recording? Do you believe it is a waiata a ringa?
   b. Possible answers include: This song appears older than "Aio" but more modern than "Waiata aroha." Like "Aio" this song is a waiata a ringa.

6. Lead students through the aural learning of "AEIOU" (see figure 5.2); you may wish to play the guitar chords along with your students as they sing.

   a. While the recording of this selection is in the key of B, it has been transcribed here in the key of D to allow for student voices and to create an easier accompaniment for the guitar. Any key you wish to sing this selection in is culturally appropriate.
   b. Dancers should step in place with one foot on the macro beat as they dance.
   c. The translation is the five vowels in Maori followed by the word *piko* (closed) and *toro* (open).

7. Once the students are able to sing the melody line, incorporate the dance movements (see figure 5.3).

   a. The entire dance should be done with hands *wiri* (trembling) both in the open and closed position. An example of the wiri can be seen in the video of waiata a ringa described above.

8. When students are secure with singing the melody line while dancing, ask them to improvise vocal harmonies above and below the melody.
9. Counting off in Maori "*Tahi . . . rua . . . toru . . . wha*" have the students do a mini-presentation of "AEIOU."

**Assessment**

1. Students may demonstrate their understanding of the material through:

   - listening and responses to discussion points.
   - singing the waiata a ringa "AEIOU."
   - dancing waiata a ringa "AEIOU."

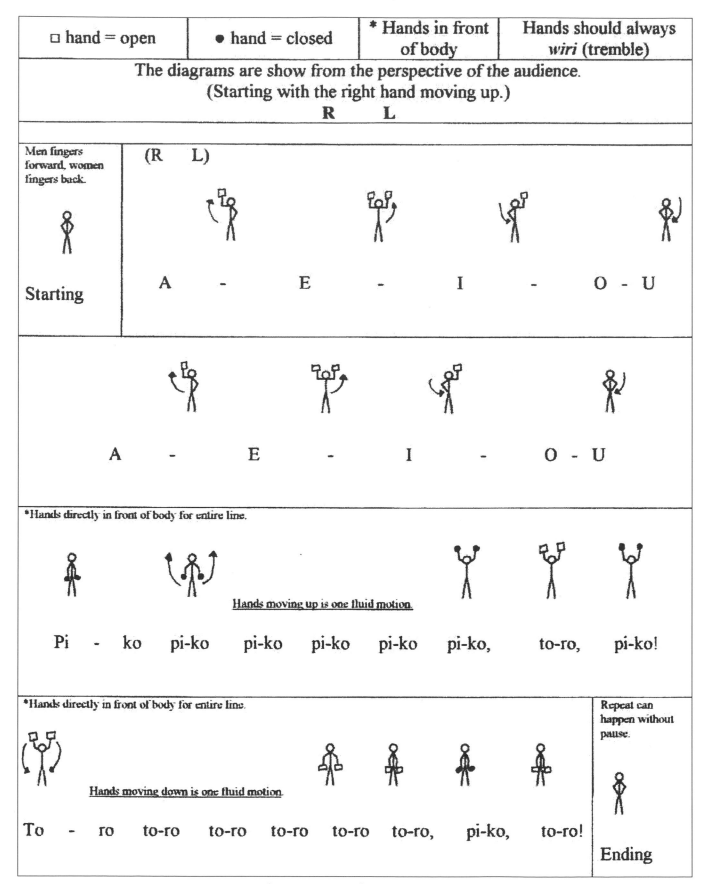

**Figure 5.3** AEIOU dance movements

**LESSON 4: SAMOAN SLIT DRUM SOUNDS AND SIGNALS (GRADES 3–8)**

**National Standards**

- Performing on instruments, alone and with others, a varied repertoire of music
- Composing and arranging music within specified guidelines
- Reading and notating music
- Listening to, analyzing, and describing music
- Understanding music in relation to history and culture

**Objectives**

Students will:

1. identify the type of instrument they hear (aerophone, chordophone, idiophone, membranophone) after listening to "Lali";
2. read and compose rhythm patterns;
3. play basic slit drum rhythm patterns.

**Materials**

1. Maps of Samoa
2. Pencil/paper
3. Photographs of slit drums
4. Rhythm pattern sheet
5. Rhythm sticks
6. Recording from Smithsonian Folkways, "Lali" (Samoa) performed by two members of Methodist Church from *Music from Western Samoa: From Conch Shell to Disco* (FW04270_102) (www.folkways.si.edu.)

**Procedures**

1. View the map of Samoa and provide important background information to students. Samoa is a group of Polynesian tropical islands in the South Pacific Ocean in a region known as "Oceania." The main languages spoken there are Samoan and English. Agriculture and fishing are two main industries of Samoa. It is important to note the difference between American Samoa and Samoa. American Samoa is a U.S. Territory and has been afforded strong economic links to the United States. Samoa is a separate entity that became an independent nation in 1967 when it reestablished independence from a United Nations trusteeship overseen by New Zealand.

   a. Maps and other information can be found at https://www.cia.gov/library/publications/the-world-factbook/index.html.

2. Ask students listen to "Lali" and ask them to pat the beat.

3. Lead a discussion with students about their experience:

   a. Example questions: Is it easy to do? Does the music speed up, slow down, or stay the same? What is the musical term for this concept?

   b. Answers: Patting a steady beat may be difficult as the music speeds up. The musical term for this phenomenon is "accelerando."

4. Ask students to identify the kinds of instrument they believe they are listening to:

   a. Possible answers include aerophones, chordophones, idiophones, and membranophones.

   b. Answer: Slit drums are classified as idiophones.

   c. While listening, invite students to think about what the slit drum might look like. Ask students to draw their ideas on a sheet of paper.

5. Discuss the slit drum (also called the slit gong) (see figure 5.4) using the following important points.

---

This lesson was contributed by Sarah Watts.

a. Slit drums are constructed from hollowed-out tree trunks. They are sometimes used to provide aural signals and other times they are used in music. It is believed that Samoan slit drums originated in Fiji. Slit drums are found in many cultures in the Pacific Islands and around the world. "Lali" is a medium-sized Samoan slit drum and is performed in pairs—*tatasi* (higher pitched of the two) and *talua* (lower pitched of the two).

b. View a photograph of the slit drum. Then, revisit students' drawings of how they imagined slit drums might look. Engage students in a discussion using the following points: Was your picture similar or different? Were you surprised to see what the slit drum really looks like?

c. Visit www.neng.usu.edu/ece/faculty/wheeler/NIU/Slitdrum.htm for a photograph and sound file of the slit drum.

d. For further reading about slit drums consult the following resources:

M. McLean, *Weavers of Song: Polynesian Music and Dance* (Honolulu, Hawaii: University of Hawaii Press, 1999).

R. Moyle, *Traditional Samoan Music* (Auckland, New Zealand: Auckland University Press, 1988).

6. Listen to "Lali" once more, paying close attention to the rhythmical patterns of the tatasi and talua.

7. Distribute rhythm sticks to students. Have students find a drumming surface such as the top of a desk, the bottom of a chair, chair legs, or a plastic bucket. Using the rhythm sticks ask students to drum along with the recording, using the basic rhythm patterns provided in figure 5.5.

The tatasi and talua slit drum rhythm patterns provided make use of quarter notes, eighth notes, and sixteenth notes in an ostinato of sorts. Discuss the concept of ostinato, a repeating pattern. The following steps are a guideline for implementing the slit drum patterns:

a. Everyone plays tatasi part along with the recording.

b. Everyone plays talua part along with the recording.

c. Split the class into a tatasi group and a talua group to play along with the recording.

d. Switch groups.

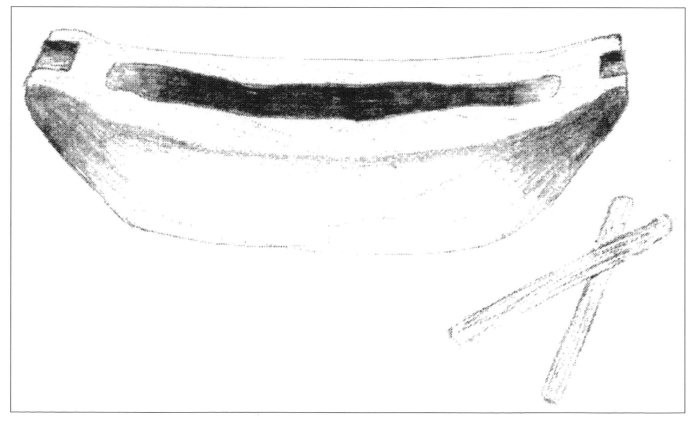

**Figure 5.4 Samoan slit drum**

**Figure 5.5  Basic slit drum patterns from "Lali"**

8. Divide the class into pairs. Each pair of students is responsible for taking quarter notes, eighth notes, and six-teenth notes and creating a four-beat rhythm pattern for a tatasi part and a talua part. Allow students to play their created patterns along with the recording.

**Assessment**

1. Students may demonstrate their understanding of the material through:
   - listening and responses to discussion points.
   - composition of four-beat slit drum ostinati.
   - rhythm stick performance.

## LESSON 5: CELEBRATORY SOUNDS OF SAMOA

**National Standards**

- Composing and arranging music within specified guidelines.
- Listening to, analyzing, and describing music.

**Objectives**

Students will:

1. listen to a recording of "Vi'i O Solo Solo" and determine what characteristics indicate that it is a celebratory song;
2. compose body percussion ostinati to accompany "Vi'i O Solo Solo."

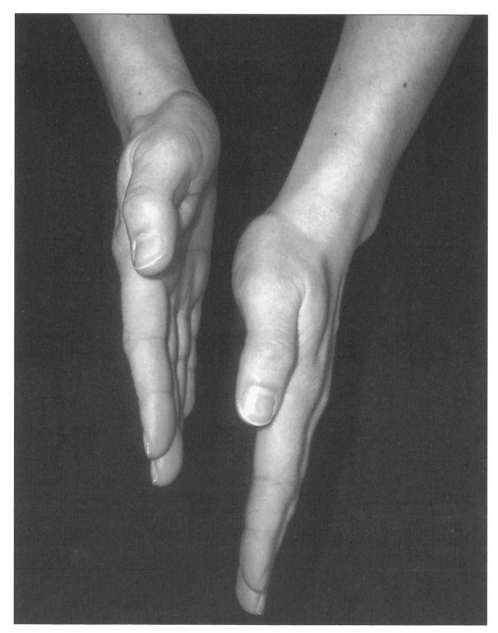

**Figure 5.6a Handclapping styles**

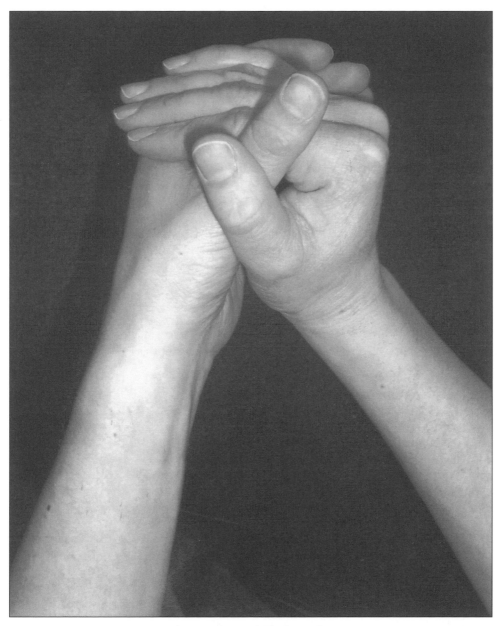

**Figure 5.6b  Handclapping styles**

## Materials

1. Recording from Smithsonian Folkways: "Vi'i O Solo Solo" performed by Matai of Solosolo, Upolu, from *Music from Western Samoa: from Conch Shell to Disco* (FW04270_106), available from www.folkways.si.edu.
2. Pencils and paper

## Procedures

1. Ask students to describe and discuss some of the ways in which music is used for celebration in their own lives. Discuss the role of music in celebrations of various kinds.
2. Listen to the recording of "Vi'i O Solo Solo" (suggested starting point, 3 minutes, 30 seconds). Ask students to pay close attention to the celebratory nature of this selection and to write down elements within the music that make them feel this selection is about a celebration. Have students share their answers with the class.

3. Begin "Vi'i O Solo Solo" again and ask students to clap along with the singers to experiment with various rhythmical patterns in an improvised way.
4. Lead a discussion on the use of handclapping in Samoan music.
   a. Various forms of body percussion may be found in traditional Samoan music. Handclapping may accompany dancing and may take on different forms. Clapping with parallel hands signifies joy or having fun. Clapping with hands cupped into right angles signifies respect. See figures 5.6a and 5.6b for a reference.
   b. Allow students to experiment with making the various handclaps. Invite them to consider: What different types of claps or body percussion sounds can you create? Can you make different sounds by incorporating the floor, your desktop, or other surfaces?
5. Compose a body percussion ostinato to perform along with the recording of "Vi'i O Solo Solo."

## Assessment

1. Students may demonstrate their understanding of the material through:
   - responses to discussion points about the celebratory nature of the recorded selection.
   - body percussion composition.

## LESSON 6: STEEL GUITAR SOUNDS OF HAWAII

### National Standards

- Listening to, analyzing, and describing music
- Understanding music in relation to history and culture

### Objectives

Students will:

1. listen to a recording of "Fair Hawai'i" in order to develop an understanding of the Hawaiian Steel Guitar sound;
2. students will respond to music through a movement activity.

### Materials

1. Recording from Smithsonian Folkways: "Fair Hawai'i" by Tony Ku and Tomomi Sugiura from *Original Hawaiian Steel Guitar* (FW08714_101), available from www.folkways.si.edu.
2. Note cards

### Procedures

1. Find Hawaii on a map of the United States and discuss its incorporation as the fiftieth state in the United States in 1959. Although it is part of the United States, it has a unique culture that features influences from various parts of the globe.
2. One of the unique musical developments in Hawaii was that of steel guitar playing. Steel guitar playing was developed by a Hawaiian man named Joseph Kekuku shortly before the turn of the twentieth century. He experimented with various ways of playing the strings of the guitar, finding that depressing the strings with a piece of metal provided the ethereal sound now associated with Hawaiian steel guitar playing.
3. Invite students to listen to "Fair Hawai'i" while quietly tapping the beats.
4. Engage students in a movement activity using "Fair Hawai'i."
   a. Using large cardstock note cards create one card that features a whole note, one card with a half note, and one card with a quarter note.
   b. Invite students to "put the beat in their feet," as they walk around the classroom while listening to the recording.
   c. Display the card that corresponds to the type of note students should show in their feet.
   d. Change the cards periodically so that students must show change in pulse with their feet.
   e. For longer note values, make sure that students are moving throughout the entire duration of the note.
   f. Once students have mastered this movement activity, invite student leaders to display the note value cards.
5. Engage students in a brief discussion—where else have you heard the sliding sounds of the steel guitar? Answers may include country music, gospel music, pop music, etc.
6. Invite students to discuss their experiences with Hawaiian culture, including pictures from vacations or other steel guitar recordings they may be familiar with.

### Assessment

1. Students may demonstrate their understanding of the material through:
   - responses to discussion points.
   - showing the correct beats in their feet.

---

This lesson was contributed by Sarah Watts.

## MUSIC ACROSS THE CURRICULUM

In order to allow students to experience music across the curriculum, teachers may be interested in including the following ideas in their lesson planning. These projects can be taught by the music teacher alone or in conjunction with other teachers in their school buildings.

1.  Building a map of the Pacific (geography). Teachers can ask students to assist in the construction of a map of the Pacific and the many islands and cultures within it. Individual students can be assigned or choose a country or series of islands that they can construct out of common materials. Students may even be encouraged to draw images upon their islands that represent the cultures that live on their assigned or chosen island. Students' islands can be displayed around the classroom in geographical locations similar to their placement around the Pacific Ocean or they can be displayed on a bulletin board. Students can find additional information on all of the island of the Pacific by exploring the CIA World Factbook at https://www.cia.gov/library/publications/the-world-factbook/.
2.  Mapping human travel across the Pacific Ocean (history and geography). Using the information provided within the chapter under the title "Mapping Pacific Island Travels" students can track the movement of people across the Pacific. Teachers may also be interested in creating an estimated timeline of movement across the pacific.
3.  Filling a *waka*, or canoe, to travel across the Pacific (social science and math). Teachers can lead students through an imaginary voyage across the Pacific. After selecting a portion of the original migration pattern used by people to cross the Pacific from one island to another, teachers can use the information provided in the "Mapping Pacific Island Travels" to guide students on an imaginary voyage between islands. Taking into consideration the typical size and speed of a traditional waka, students will need to determine how many boats are needed to take their class on this voyage. They will also need to determine how long it will take their class to arrive at their new destination, what provisions would be needed and can fit upon their vessels, and which provisions would be most beneficial for the voyage. This project provides a great opportunity to work with the school's social science and math teachers.
4.  Mapping the sea and sky (science). Pacific peoples' travels have often been navigated by evaluation of sea currents, sea conditions, and astronomy. Teachers may elect to include a project that allows students an opportunity to evaluate sea conditions and patterns or look at star maps of the northern and southern hemispheres. This lesson provides an opportunity to incorporate the expertise of the school's science teacher. Information regarding ocean currents can be found at www.oscar.noaa.gov/ (the National Oceanic and Atmospheric Association) and information regarding star mapping can be found at www.nasa.gov/audience/foreducators/index.html (Science at the National Aeronautics and Space Administration). Additional information geared specifically for teachers and classroom use can be found at http://earthsky.org/space.
5.  Comparing visual arts (visual arts and social studies). The multiple cultures found across the Pacific offer an excellent opportunity for students to explore the visual arts as they are related to the cultures that produce them. Teachers may be interested in working with the school's art teacher to provide students an opportunity to view different works of art from around the Pacific and to experiment with their own replication of these art styles and forms. For example students may be presented with pictures of Maori *mahi raranga* (weaving) and then be given an opportunity to create their own weaving using simple materials such as strips of construction paper in various traditional colors. Information on Maori weaving and images may be found at www.liverpoolmuseums.org.uk/wml/humanworld/worldcultures/oceania/newzealand/Weaving.asp. Teachers can then present images of Indigenous Australian art, which can be found at http://aboriginalart.com.au/, then allow students an opportunity to create a ground mosaic that is constructed by the entire class out of various colors of sand. Reproductions of theses visual art forms should be guided to insure students understand the cultural meaning of these art forms.

## NOTE

1.  Download a map of Oceania from *National Geographic* (www.nationalgeographic.com/xpeditions/atlas/) and project it on a screen for the students.

# FILMOGRAPHY

## Pacific at Large

*Dances of Life.* 60-minute DVD. Produced by PBS.
*Pilot Guide to the Pacific: Fiji, Vanuatu, and Solomon Islands.* 45-minute DVD. Produced by Lonely Planet Pilot Guides.
*Ring of Fire Imax.* 40-minute DVD, 1991. Produced by the Graphics Film Corporation.

## Australia

*Dance on Your Land.* 28-minute DVD, 1991. Produced by the Woomera Aboriginal Cooperation.
*Discovery Atlas Australia.* 100-minute DVD. Produced by the Discovery Channel.

## Hawaii

*Children of the Long Canoes: A Unique History of Hawaii.* 55-minute videotape, color, 1991. Produced by the Albert and Trudy Kallis Foundation.
*Everything You Wanted to Know about Hawaiian Hula.* 80-minute videotape, color, 1990. Produced by Shamani Enterprises, Ft. Myers, Fla.
*Hula Auwana: Modern Hawaiian Dance.* 20-minute videotape, color, 1986. Produced by the Hawaii State Department of Education.
*Hula Kahiko: Traditional Hawaiian Dance.* 20-minute videotape, color, 1986. Produced by the Hawaii State Department of Education.
*Hula Pai: Hula Beat.* 15-minute videotape, color, 1989. Produced by LPIM, Ft. Collins, Colo.
*The Kamaka Ukulele. Olelo Hawaii. The Saltmakers. Keiki Hula.* 30-minute videotape, color, 1987. Produced by Juniroa Productions, Honolulu.
*Keiki Hula.* 45-minute videotape, color, 1989. Produced by LPIM, Fort Collins, Colo.
*Language Is the Root.* 29-minute videotape, color, 1984. Produced by Hawaii Public Television, Honolulu.
*Na Mea Hookani: Instruments of the Hula.* 20-minute video, color, 1987. Produced by the Hawaii State Department of Education.
*Pele. Dante Carpenter, Mayor of Hawaii. Puuhonua-o-Honaunau. Moki's Music.* 30-minute videotape, 1986. Produced by Juniroa Productions, Honolulu.
*Queen Liliuokalani (1838–1917), the Last Ruling Hawaiian Monarch.* 13-minute videotape, color, 1992. Produced by the Northeast Metro Minnesota Branch, American Association of University Women, Shoreview, Minn.
*Secret Blossoms: Na Pua Hana.* 24-minute videotape, color, 1993. Produced by Green Glass Productions.
*You Can Do the Hula.* 37-minute videotape, 1986. Produced by Rainforest Publishing, Honolulu.

## Maori (New Zealand)

*Heritage of Maori Song.* 54-minutes, DVD, 2007. Produced by Viking.
*Live and Proud: Maona and the Tribe.* 65-minutes with added features, 2007. Produced by Rajon.
*New Zealand to the Max.* 79-minute DVD, 2007. Produced by Small Wonders Productions.
*Te Hekenga-a-rangi: Hirini Melbourn and Richard Nuns in Concert.* CD and DVD boxed set, 2003. Producer Steven Garden.
*Te Vaka "Live at Apia Park."* 96-minute DVD with added features. Produced by Te Vaka.
*Whale Rider.* 101-minute DVD with added features, 2002. Produced by ApolloMedia, Auckland, New Zealand.

## Samoa

Multiple Samoan videos can be streamed for free over the Internet from the following website: www.samoanmusicandvideo.com/index.php?option=com_content&task=category&sectionid=6&id=25&Itemid=54.

*Globe Trekker Destination Tahiti and Samoa Travel Guide.* 60-minute DVD, 2004. Produced by Globe Trekker.
*Horizons/WTP/FAA Soma.* 60-minute DVD, 2004. Produced by the Polynesian Cultural Center, Laie, Hawaii.
*We Call Samoa Home.* 23-minute videotape, 1989. Produced by the Christian World Service, Christchurch, New Zealand.
*World Fireknife Championship.* 46-Minutes, 2006. Produced by the Polynesian Cultural Center, Laie, Hawaii.

## Internet Resources

*Pacific at Large*

Apple iTunes, www.apple.com/itunes/
Calabash, www.calabashmusic.com/
CIA World Factbook, https://www.cia.gov/library/publications/the-world-factbook/

C/Net Download, http://music.download.com/
E-Music, http://emusic.com
Global Rhythm, www.globalrhythm.net/
Music India Online, www.musicindiaonline.com/
Napster, www.napster.com
Rhapsody, www.rhapsody.com
Smithsonian Global Sounds, www.smithsonianglobalsound.org/

## Australia

Australian Music Resources, www.amws.com.au/
Aboriginal Art and Culture Center, http://aboriginalart.com.au/
Australian Government Cultural Portal, www.cultureandrecreation.gov.au/articles/music/
Australian Music Center, www.amcoz.com.au/
Australian Music Online, www.amo.org.au/
Indigenous Australia, www.indig.com/
National Library of Australia and Soundscreen, www.musicaustralia.org/

## Hawai'i

Hawaiian Culture Index, www.alternative-hawaii.com/hacul/
Hawaiian History, www.hawaiihistory.org/
Hawaiian Music and Hula Archives, www.huapala.org/
Hawaiian Music Store, www.hawaiianmusicstore.com/
Hula Lessons and Activities, www.realhula.com/

## Maori (New Zealand)

Maori Culture and History, www.newzealand.com/travel/about-nz/culture/culture-maori-culture.cfm
Maori Culture and Music, www.maori.org.nz/
Maori Haka Interactive, www.newzealand.com/travel/about-nz/features/haka-feature/haka.cfm
Maori History, http://history-nz.org/maori.html
New Zealand Folksongs, http://folksong.org.nz/

## Samoa

American Samoa, www.amsamoa.net/
Samoa, www.samoa.co.uk/music&culture.html

# BIBLIOGRAPHY

## Pacific at Large

Hayward, P. *Sound Alliances: Indigenous Peoples, Cultural Politics and Popular Music in the Pacific*. London, England: Wellington House, 1998.
Malm, W. P. *Music Cultures of the Pacific, the Near East, and Asia*. Upper Saddle River, N.J.: Simon and Schuster, 1996.

## Australia

Breen, M., ed. *Our Place, Our Music*. Canberra: Aboriginal Studies Press, 1989.
Castles, J. "Tjungaringanyi: Aboriginal Rock." In *From Pop to Punk to Postmodernism*, edited by P. Hayward, 25–39. Sydney: Allen and Unwin, 1992.
Dunbar-Hall, P. "'Alive and Deadly': A Sociolinguistic Reading of Rock Songs by Australian Aboriginal Musicians." *Popular Music and Society* 27, no. 1 (2004): 41–48.
———. "Religious Traditions of Aboriginal Peoples." In *Music! Its Role and Importance in Our Lives*, edited by G. DeGraffenried, C. Fowler, T. Gerber, and V. Lawrence, 244–46. New York: McGraw-Hill/Glencoe, 2006.

———. "Technologising Culture: Access, Control and Aboriginal Knowledge." *Proceedings of the International Society for Music Education 24th World Conference, Edmonton, Canada,* 2000, 98–104.

———. "'We Have Survived': Popular Music as Representation of Australian Aboriginal Cultural Loss and Reclamation." In *The Resisting Muse: Popular Music and Social Protest,* edited by I. Peddie, 119–31. London: Ashgate, 2006.

Dunbar-Hall, P., and C. Gibson. *Deadly Sounds, Deadly Places: Contemporary Aboriginal Music in Australia.* Sydney: UNSW Press, 2004.

Gibson, C., and P. Dunbar-Hall. "Mediating Contemporary Aboriginal Music: Discussions of the Music Industry in Australia." *Perfect Beat* 7.1 (2005): 17–41.

———. "Nitmiluk: Place, Politics and Empowerment in Australian Aboriginal Popular Music." In *Ethnomusicology: A Contemporary Reader,* edited by J. Post, 383–400. London: Routledge, 2006.

———. "Nitmiluk: Place and Empowerment in Australian Aboriginal Popular Music." *Ethnomusicology* 44, no. 1 (2000): 39–64.

Lawrence, G. *Traditionalism and Modernity in the Music and Dance of Oceania: Essays in Honour of Barbara B. Smith.* Sydney: University of Sydney, 2001.

Marett, A. *Songs, Dreaming, and Ghosts: The Wangga of North Australia.* Middletown, Conn.: Wesleyan University Press, 2005.

Richards, F., ed. *The Soundscapes of Australia.* Hampshire, England: Ashgate Publishing Limited, 2007.

Walker, C. *Buried Country.* Sydney: Pluto Press, 2000.

## Hawaii

Kaeppler, A. L. *Hula Pahu: Hawaiian Drum Dances.* Honolulu: Bishop Museum Press, 1993.

Kanahele, G. S. *Hawaiian Music and Musicians: An Illustrated History.* Honolulu: University of Hawaii Press, 1979.

Stoneburner, B. C. *Hawaiian Music: An Annotated Bibliography.* New York: Greenwood Press, 1986.

## Maori (New Zealand)

Flinton, B. *Taonga Puoro: Singing Treasures—the Musical Instruments of the Maori.* Auckland, New Zealand: Craig Potton Publishing, 2004.

Karetu, T. *Haka! The Dance of a Noble People.* Auckland, New Zealand: Raupo Publishing, 1993.

McLean, M. *Maori Music: Records and Analysis of Ancient Maori Musical Traditions and Knowledge.* Auckland, New Zealand: Auckland University Press, 1997.

———. *To Tatau Waka: In Search of Maori Music, 1958–1979.* Auckland, New Zealand: Auckland University Press, 2004.

Ngata, R., and A. Armstrong. *Maori Action Songs: Words and Music, Actions and Instructions.* Auckland, New Zealand: Raupo Publishing, 2002.

## Samoa

McLean, M. *Weavers of Song: Polynesian Music and Dance.* Honolulu: University of Hawaii Press, 1999.

Moyle, R. *Polynesian Music and Dance.* Auckland, New Zealand: Centre for Pacific Studies, 1991.

———. *Traditional Samoan Music.* Auckland, New Zealand: Auckland University Press, 1988.

Sapolu, T. A. *The Iao and Her Nest.* Pago Pago, American Samoa: Samoa New, 1997.

Schaefer, L. M. *An Island Grows.* New York: Greenwillow Books, 2006.

# 6

## World Beat

*Patricia Shehan Campbell and David G. Hebert*

World beat, a subset of the commercial music category known as world music, is a term referring to music that fuses folk and traditional music with Western rock and pop influences.[1] The genre brings to mind the powerful musical energy of such megastars as Ladysmith Black Mambazo (the South African men's choir with its resonant and pulsive vocal quality), Ivo Papasov (the Bulgarian bebop clarinetist with his virtuosic and jazz-style improvisations), Gilberto Gil (the founder of tropicalismo, that Brazilian blend of regional and rock elements), Thomas Mapfumo (the proverbial lion of Zimbabwe and his flood of electric *mbira* music), Ofra Haza (the Israeli pop singer of Yemeni folk songs with a beat), and Nusrat Fateh Ali Khan (the legendary *qawwali* singer of Pakistan). Riverdance and the Buena Vista Social Club are further examples of world beat, the musical phenomenon that has rocked the world of music and sent its listeners into reactions that range from dancing frenzy to blissful contemplation.

Like world music, world beat emerged as a category of music in the mid-1980s. It may have existed prior to that, but there is general agreement that the floodgates opened wide in the United Kingdom and the United States at about this time to embrace the concept of folk-and-rock fusion. The name caught on as record companies signed artists who were adding a beat to their instrumental and vocal music traditions, and festivals became the forums for their performances in London, Sydney, Rio de Janeiro, Berlin, New York, and Seattle. Artists-turned-producers like David Byrne, Paul Simon, and Peter Gabriel fanned the fire, and gave their support to the world beat artists and festivals, and did well themselves to incorporate influences of the world's music into their own expressions.

World beat embraces nearly any style (except Appalachian folk music), and is especially keyed to the blend of popular music with folk and "roots" music of the African continent and across Latin America. Yet world beat can appear anywhere—in China, Ireland, India, Egypt, Korea, Bulgaria, Thailand, Turkey, the Pacific Islands, and the Arctic Circle—as a musical phenomenon that adds a decided "groove" (and often Western rock instruments) to music that nonetheless is "folk," rustic, rural, or traditional in character. Notable examples of world beat include Juju, Bhangra, Pop-Rai, and Zouk. World beat transcends genre names in that the blend of pop with folk influences is often unnamed but decidedly present.

Among the various indigenous traditions that have sprung into the realm of world beat are those of communities in the southern Pacific, Ireland, among the Inuit of Nunavut, the Yukon, and Alaska, and across the African subcontinent. Inventive artists drawn to pop music sensibilities have found the groove that fits their music best, including bands known as Te Vaka, Nesian Mystik, Altan, Tudjaat, Afrocelts, and Zap Mama. Much of the music of Oceania, living on islands and atolls spread across Polynesia, Melanesia, and Micronesia, is a fusion of indigenous elements with European secular and religious music—along with the more recent impact of American pop, rock, and hip-hop styles. In Ireland and across the Celtic world, "roots"-styled folk, blending fiddles and flutes with electric guitars and amped bodhrans, hold wide appeal to listeners in concerts and clubs. Native American musicians have crossed over to mainstream popular styles for some time, playing in country and rock bands, and also adapting old traditional forms with acoustic folk styles, electronics, and even forging meditative music at the far end of creative invention. As for the fusion that has taken the world by storm, Afro-pop or Afro-beat, the rhythms, melodies, and musical textures of the African continent (particularly West, East, and southern Africa) have been engaging listeners to dance for decades now. The origins of world beat began with Afro-pop, in fact, and its multiple expressive styles today are a development of the early fusion that transpired when the roots of African music met rock. World beat is a sign of the times, a result of a world that is connected by telecommunication that brings people from all corners of the world in touch with one another, at which point influences combine to make for new artistic expressions.

## LESSON 1: PACIFIC ISLAND FUSION

### National Standards

- Singing, alone and with others, a varied repertoire of music
- Performing on instruments, alone and with others, a varied repertoire of music
- Listening to, analyzing, and describing music
- Understanding relationships between music, the other arts, and disciplines outside the arts

### Objectives

Students will:

1. understand the role of indigenous Polynesian instruments in this music, including the nose flute, pate (log drum), and ukulele;
2. learn about the role of diverse Pacific cultures within the band Te Vaka;
3. understand the meaning of the song lyrics to "Tutuki";
4. learn to sing "Tutuki";
5. explore possibilities for dancing the fatele.

### Materials

1. Recording and lyrics of "Tutuki" from the following albums or online resources:
   - *Te Vaka*, "Tutuki" (2004, Spirit of Play Productions), available on iTunes
   - Te Vaka official website, www.tevaka.com/
2. Recording of Pacific "Fangufangu Nose Flute," available on iTunes
3. Photo, downloadable at http://en.wikipedia.org/wiki/Image:Joueur_de_vivio.jpg
4. Film: Tuvaluan "Fatele" dance, available on www.youtube.com

### Procedures

1. Listen to a recording of "Tutuki" by the Polynesian world beat band, Te Vaka, and find answers to the following questions: What part of the world does the music come from? (Answer: Polynesia.) What instruments do they hear? (Answers: voices, ukulele, guitar, pate [log drums], clapping.) How are the instruments played? (Answers: The lutes—guitar and ukulele—are strummed, and the log drums are played by wood mallets.)
2. Play a recording of Polynesian fangufangu nose flute, available on iTunes. After opportunities for students guessing the type of instrument that plays its melody at a very soft dynamic level, show a picture of a nose flute (www.images.google.com, Polynesian nose flute).
3. Allow students an opportunity to respond to the photograph of the musicians, with attention to the nose flute and the upside-down metal pot. Explain the origins of the photo over a century ago on the island of Tahiti in the southern Pacific. The nose flute is still occasionally played for lullabies, and its soft quality requires an intimate "chamber" environment.
4. Play again the recording of "Tutuki" and allow students an opportunity to contemplate the musical reality of nose flutes and rock bands in the same region of the Pacific. While nose flutes are rarely heard, the dance music genres of the Pacific peoples—in Polynesia, Melanesia, and Micronesia—are appealing to listeners in the region and across the world. Clarify that "Tutuki" is identifiably Pacific due to the use of the log drum and choral harmony, and an example of world beat with its blend of guitar and high-tech recording quality that amplifies and underscores its function as a dance music selection.
5. Listen again to "Tutuki" and identity the meter (duple) and frequent presence of syncopations. Try tapping the accented and unaccented pulses, and imitate some of the syncopated rhythms.
6. Follow the Tokelauan words of "Tutuki," composed by Te Vaka band leader Opetaia Foa'i. Share also the English translation of the verses, and discuss the meaning of the dance to Pacific Island peoples, as expressed in the song (see lyrics on website or CD sleeve).

This lesson was prepared by David G. Hebert and Patricia Shehan Campbell.

7. Over the course of several listenings, orally learn to sing the words with the melody.

8. Show an example of fatele, the dance, available on www.youtube.com. Challenge students to imitate some of the moves, and to even develop some of them into a "modified classroom" version of fatele.

9. Direct students to the website of Te Vaka, the performers of "Tutuki." They can glean details of the band, directed by the following questions. How large is Te Vaka? (Answer: ten members, including singers, instrumentalists, and dancers.) What cultures do Te Vaka members represent? (Answer: various Pacific Island groups, including Tokelau, Tuvalu, Samoa, Cook Islands, and New Zealand.) Who is the band leader? (Answer: Opetaia Foa'I, a Tuvaluan.) What are the highlights and successes of the band? (Answer: They have released five internationally acclaimed albums and two DVDs; have performed in over thirty countries; have been nominated for two BBC Radio 3 World Music Awards; are recipients of Best International Achievement Award for "Ki mua" in 1999, the Best Roots Album for *Nukukehe* in 2003 and Best Pacific Music Album for *Tutuki* in 2004 in the New Zealand Music Industry Awards and Best Pacific Music Album for *Olatia* in 2008.) What languages does Te Vaka sing in? (Answer: The band leader, Opetaia Foa'I, speaks English, Samoan, Tuvaluan, and Tokelauan, and usually sings in Tokelauan.)

## Assessment

1. Sing the song(s) with accurate pitches, rhythm, and words.
2. Identify and describe traditional Polynesian elements in this music (fatele, pate, ukulele).
3. Discuss the importance of movement and dance in Pacific Island culture.

## LESSON 2: PACIFIC ISLAND HIP-HOP

### National Standards

- Listening to, analyzing, and describing music
- Evaluating music and music performances
- Understanding relationships between music, the other arts, and disciplines outside the arts

### Objectives

Students will:

1. learn about the role of hip-hop in Polynesian youth cultural identity;
2. analyze and describe an example of cross-cultural musical fusion.

### Materials

1. Recordings and lyrics of Nesian Mystik from the Nesian Mystik official website, www.nesian-mystik.com/
2. Additional Internet resources are also recommended:
   - Flava: *Hip Hop, RnB* (New Zealand/Polynesian Radio), www.flava.co.nz/
   - Maori Music, www.maorimusic.com
3. Sticks (wood rhythm sticks)
4. Drums of various sizes and shapes

### Procedures

1. Play a recording of "Nesian Style" for students to listen to, with the intent of soliciting discussion on the concept of hip-hop gone global. Challenge students to think about similarities and distinctions between this example of hip-hop and styles they know well.
   Ask them to comment on reasons why hip-hop, an American popular music expression (initially African American) has found its way into popular music in New Zealand.
2. Listen again to "Nesian Style," asking students to find the pulse and to keep it by tapping, patting, or clapping it.
3. Introduce Nesian Mystik as a Polynesian hip-hop band from New Zealand that has received numerous awards. Display lyrics from the band website, asking students to read for any unfamiliar words that need explanation. Facilitate discussion on segments that express Polynesian pride, or identity, and those that refer to aspects of music ("rocking mics," "vocalists") and dance ("shaking them hips").
4. Distribute sticks and drums, and encourage students to play the pulse, and to pick up by ear and play a rhythmic ostinato, as they listen to "Nesian Style" again.
5. Encourage students to sing (chant) along with the repeating chorus section.
6. Engage in a class discussion of hip-hop in the United States and abroad. What kinds of positive and negative messages are conveyed through hip-hop? What kinds of skills are needed in order to succeed at freestyling and battle rhyming? To what extent are these musical skills, or are they also language arts skills?

### Assessment

1. Identify aspects of both Polynesian and global hip-hop cultures evident in this recorded selection.
2. Explain the role of hip-hop in youth cultural identity.

---

This lesson was prepared by David G. Hebert.

## LESSON 3: BRINGING THE BEAT TO IRISH TRADITIONS

### National Standards

- Singing, alone and with others, a varied repertoire of music
- Performing on instruments, alone and with others, a varied repertoire of music
- Listening to, analyzing, and describing music

### Objectives

Students will:

1. listen to the song "Dulaman" and tap the beat of the bodhran;
2. sing the melody of the refrain on a neutral syllable, and with the Gaelic lyrics;
3. play a basic bodhran (drum) pattern;
4. play the melody on available instruments such as flute, recorder, violin;
5. play the chords on guitar;
6. compare two recorded versions of "Brid Og Ni Mhaille."

### Materials

1. Recordings: "Dulaman," featuring Altan, Island Angel, available from iTunes; "Brid Og Ni Mhaille," featuring Altan, Island Angel, available from iTunes; "Brid Og Ni Mhaille," featuring Deirdre Ni Fhilionn, *Irish Traditional Songs*, Smithsonian Folkways
2. "Dulaman," featuring Altan, available on www.youtube.com
3. Altan website, www.altan.ie/
4. Music notation for "Dulaman" (*Tunes and Grooves*, p. 105)
5. Bodhran drums, or other hand drums
6. Melody instruments such as flute, recorder, violin, concertina

### Procedures

1. Listen to "Dulaman," and ask students to keep the steady pulse that is sounded by guitar and drum. Counting a fast "1-2-3 4-5-6," ask students to listen again to the recording and to pat six beats (with palms of the hand on any surface, or just the tapping of two fingers if a softer quality is desired). Challenge them to find a way to pat or tap more strongly on beats 1 and 4:

   | 1 | 2 | 3 | 4 | 5 | 6 |
   |---|---|---|---|---|---|
   | X |   |   | X |   |   |

3. Listening again, direct students to the verse-refrain, or AB, form of the song. Distribute hand drums, or the flat Irish traditional drum known as bodhran, and ask students to play the fast six beats, with first and fourth beat accents on the drums.
4. Sing the melody of the refrain on a neutral syllable such as *la* (see figure 6.1).
5. Provide a translation of the Gaelic words for the recurring refrain in this traditional children's song about the sea and seaweed: "Seaweed from the yellow cliff, Irish seaweed, Seaweed from the ocean: The best in all of Ireland!"
6. Learn to sing by ear, through multiple listenings, the Gaelic words of the song's refrain.
7. Practice various possible accompaniment patterns on bodhran, with the intent of switching between patterns, combining patterns—even improvising on them—as the recording plays.

   | Count: | 1-2-3 4-5-6 |
   |---|---|
   | Drum pattern 1: | 6 eighth notes |
   | 2: | quarter eighth, quarter eighth |
   | 3 | 2 dotted quarters |
   | 4: | 3 eighth notes, dotted quarter |
   | 5: | quarter eighth, 3 eighth notes |

This lesson was prepared by Patricia Shehan Campbell.

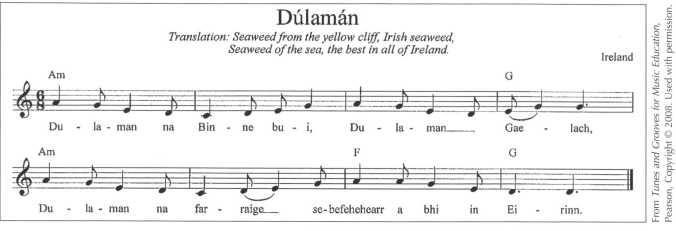

**Figure 6.1 "Dulaman"**

8. Play the melody on flute, violin, concertina, or other melody instrument.
9. Play the chords on guitar or piano, sounding them on beats one and four, while singing the melody. Explore the possibilities for a fast, arpeggiated, broken-chord accompaniment.
10. Watch the band on www.youtube.com, performing in a live concert. Ask students to identify the instruments they hear (voice, fiddles, guitars, bodhran, concertina), and to comment on the culture of the live-concert version of "Dulaman."
11. Assign students the task of finding out about the Irish world beat group Altan.
    Ask them to seek answers to these questions: Where is the band Altan from? (Answer: Ireland, in the northwestern county of Donegal.) How many players are in Altan? (Answer: six, including singer-fiddle player Mairead Ni Mhaonaigh, who is featured on two of the songs in this lesson.) What is the instrumental mix of the band? (Answer: several guitars, fiddles, a bouzouki [another plucked lute, like a guitar but with a long neck], concertina.) Where did the band's name come from? (Answer: There is a lake in Donegal called Loch Altan.)
12. To explore the roots of a traditional song that becomes an expression of a popular Irish world beat band, listen to two versions of "Brid Og Ni Mhaille." The earlier version of these is performed by singer Deirdre Ni Fhlionn in 1958, with Irish harp accompaniment, and Altan performs the second version in the 1990s, with the singer backed by guitar and synthesizer and high-quality recording technique. Ask students to determine their favorite version of this song (about a young man who is left broken-hearted after his secret love, Brid (Bridget) Og Ni Mhaille, marries another), and to explain why. Likely, they will speak to the sharper sound quality and more contemporary vocal styling (with lower range and lack of vibrato) as appealing to their modern sensibilities.
13. Find Ireland, and County Donegal, on a map of Europe or of the world. As it was more isolated from the Irish capital, Dublin, this region retained the Gaelic language and culture to a greater extent than other areas of the country.

**Assessment**

1. Sing the refrain to the Irish traditional song "Dulaman."
2. Accurately play the pulse and appropriate rhythmic patterns to "Dulaman" on bodhran or hand drums.
3. Play the melody to the refrain (and verse) of "Dulaman," on melody instruments.
4. Describe the difference between a traditional and contemporary performance of an Irish folk song.

## LESSON 4: ARCTIC GROOVE

### National Standards

1. Singing, alone and with others, a varied repertoire of music
2. Performing on instruments, alone and with others, a varied repertoire of music
3. Listening to, analyzing, and describing music

### Objectives

Students will:

1. listen to the musical selection "Qiugaviit";
2. sing the melody on a neutral syllable, adding the word "Qiugaviit" as it appears;
3. play the ongoing pulse on hand drum;
4. play chordal harmony for the song on guitar or piano;
5. listen to and view other examples of songs from the indigenous northern reaches of North America, particularly the throat-singing of the Inuit.

### Materials

1. Recordings: "Qiugaviit," available from iTunes; "Potlatch Song" and "Wolf Song," from the *Anthology of North American Indian and Eskimo Music* (Smithsonian Folkways); "Swing Your Drum" and "Drum Song," from *Eskimo Songs from Alaska* (Smithsonian Folkways)
2. Films: *Inuit Throat Singing: Kathy Kettler and Karin Kettler* (Smithsonian Global Sound Live); *Inuit Throat Singing: Kathy Keknek and Janet Aglukkaq* (long), available on www.youtube.com
3. Music notation for "Qiugaviit" (*Tunes and Grooves*, p. 298)
4. Hand drums
5. Guitar, piano

### Procedures

1. Listen to "Qiugaviit." Draw students' attention to the sounds of the wind, the caribou-skin drum, the accordion, the electric guitar, and the singers. How many of these components can they identify in an initial listening experience?
2. Listen again to "Qiugaviit," this time tapping the pulse of the drum while tracking by ear the rise and fall of the melody, often seconds and thirds. Note that the singers are two Inuit women from Nunavat, Canada, who call themselves Tudjaat (Madeleine Allakariallak and Phoebe Atagotaaluk), and who sing straight and in the traditional throat-singing style.
3. Sing the melody on a neutral syllable (such as "ah"). Ask that students join in, as they can. Note that the first two phrases are the same, and the third phrase descends as contrast to the ascending first and second phrases (see figure 6.2).
4. Add the text to the song, "Qiugaviit," broken into the sung syllables, "quay-yoo-yah-way." This Inuit word translates as "Do you know now?" a question once raised by an Inuit elder to a man who went hunting without dressing for the cold, and nearly froze to death.
5. Play the ongoing pulse on hand drum, and add chords on guitar or piano, strummed or rolled once per measure as the chords change.
6. Listen to examples of songs of the Inuit (formerly called Eskimo) on the Smithsonian Folkways recordings *American Indian* and *Eskimo Music and Eskimo Song from Alaska*. Focus on the qualities of the singing voices, the timbre of the large handheld drums, the range of the melody, the repeated pitches and rhythms. Ask students to listen before knowing the title of the song, and to guess what the subject of the song might be: "What might the singers be communicating? Why do you think this?" Then, on knowing the song name, have students listen for the nuances that are intended by the performers to express the song's subject: "Is there any indication in the

---

This lesson was prepared by Patricia Shehan Campbell.

**Figure 6.2 "Qiugaviit"**

performance that this is a song for a wolf (in 'Wolf Song')? "How are the drums swinging?" "Can you describe or demonstrate the drum swing?"

7. View films on Inuit throat-singing as exemplar of a unique singing style by people in the arctic region, and discuss how the sound is produced. Listen for phonation, that is, the sound of sustained pitches, as opposed to the percussive sound of the breath that is inhaled and exhaled. The throat-singers on the Smithsonian Global Sound Live talk about the meaning of the genre to them, how the genre historically functioned as entertainment for the women when the men were hunting, as well as a means of lulling their babies to sleep.

8. Experiment with the possibilities of throat-singing, by producing sound by the breath as opposed to actual sung pitches.

9. Listen again to "Qiugaviit," after having heard the examples of indigenous North American, especially Inuit, singers. Discuss how varied the styles are, and why "Qiugaviit" sounds so much more contemporary than the others. Facilitate students to come to a discovery of the importance of advances in audio technology that provide the high quality sound of the wind, the vibration of the hide drum, the vocal nuances, and the clarity of instruments such as concertina and electric guitar.

10. Find a map of the "top of the world," the northern reaches of land near the Arctic Circle. See especially the northern parts of the North American landmass, in Canada and the United States, especially Nunavut, the Yukon, and Alaska, as regions in which the Inuit people reside and preserve their cultural traditions as they also adapt to and merge with contemporary practices.

## Assessment

1. Sing the song "Qiugaviit" accurately in tune and in time.
2. Accompany the song on hand drum, guitar, and/or piano.
3. Listen and view examples of Inuit singing, including throat-singing.
4. Compare older and world beat styles of singing in Inuit culture.

## LESSON 5: WORLD FUSION

### National Standards

- Singing, alone and with others, a varied repertoire of music
- Listening to, analyzing, and describing music
- Evaluating music and music performances
- Understanding relationships between music, the other arts, and disciplines outside the arts

### Objectives

Students will:

1. learn to identify the sounds of various traditional instruments within a world beat fusion ensemble recording;
2. learn about cultural diversity in European urban centers;
3. learn to sing and simultaneously move to "Bandy Bandy."

### Materials

1. Recording of "Whirl-y-Reel 1 (Beard and Sandals Mix)" from the following albums or online resources: Afro-Celt Sound System, vol.1, *Sound Magic* (1996), available from iTunes; Afrocelts official website, www.afrocelts.org/
2. Recording and lyrics of "Bandy Bandy" from the following albums or online resources: Zap Mama, *Bandy Bandy* EP (2005, V2 Music), available from iTunes; Zap Mama official websites: www.zapmama.com/ or www.zapmama.be/

### Procedures

1. Play the selection, "Whirl-y-Reel 1 (Beard and Sandals Mix)" by the Afrocelts, asking students to show the beat in their body (by clapping, tapping, grooving).
2. Engage students in a discussion of African migrants in Europe. Ask them, "Did you know that there are many African people in Europe?" Note that in many large urban centers of Europe—Paris, Brussels, and Lisbon, for example—there are large communities of African immigrants. Most of these communities formed relatively recently compared with African Americans, and they maintain customs and practices that are even more closely linked to specific African cultures. Dance club musicians in Europe have benefited greatly from their close proximity to these traditions, and many African musical elements have been adopted into recent dance music styles from Europe.
3. Ask students to imagine the sound style that would come from the merger of Celtic (Irish, Scottish, Gaelic) traditional music and West African styles. What instruments might they expect to hear? How might the melody, rhythm, texture sound?
4. Introduce The Afrocelts, previously known as Afro Celt Sound System, a unique world beat ensemble. Ask students to identify various instruments from Ireland and Africa within this song according to their sounds:
    a. Dundun, the "talking drum" from Africa (0:32, 1:14, etc.)
    b. Kora, a harp from West Africa (0:47, 1:02, etc.)
    c. Electric bass (0:42, 0:50, etc.)
    d. Banjo, for just a few seconds (1:33)
    e. Electronic drums (crescendo) (1:45)
    f. Tin whistle, a flute from Ireland, playing a reel (2:10)

    Since some of these instruments may not be known to students, send the students to the Internet to seek out images to be shared with the class.
5. In another listening, have students "air-play" the instruments as they appear and are featured on the selection. In other words, encourage them to "mime" the performance of the talking drum and the harp, and so on, using their gestures and movement to show that they can identify the instrument type.
6. Ask students to sort out which parts of "Whirl-y-Reel" are Celtic and which are African in origin.
7. Play a second selection of African-blended music, "Bandy Bandy," by Zap Mama. Ask students to listen carefully to the sung words, and to guess the animal about which the singers sing. The title and the refrain are clues, as "bandy" is a snake that waves its body.

---

This lesson was prepared by David G. Hebert.

8. Listening again, ask students to "wave" their hands, fingers closed and pointed, like the wriggling of a snake. Allow them to work their wave into their entire arms, first one and then the other.

9. Show the official video of "Bandy Bandy," available on www.youtube.com. Discuss the group Zap Mama and in particular the founder and leader, Marie Daulne, who was born in the Congo (once a colony of Belgium) and then moved to Belgium, where she grew up. Only as an adult did she return to the Congo to learn the music of her heritage.

10. Invite students to sing "Bandy Bandy," displaying its lyrics from the website.

## Assessment

1. Ask the students to identify particular instruments and musical forms (and their cultural origins) in the music of the Afrocelts.

2. Sing "Bandy Bandy" with accurate pitches, rhythm, and words.

## MUSIC ACROSS THE CURRICULUM

The following are some suggestions for how lessons in world beat may be extended into other academic areas:

1. Assemble students in small groups to explore the phenomenon of world beat. Where did it come from? Why has it evolved? What connections can be made between the phenomenon of musical fusion and the international shift by world leaders from insular, independent, and singular nations to political units with shared interests? How is the World Trade Organization (WTO) evolving during the same era of globalization as world beat, in a way the result of similar political and economic influences?

2. Students can be directed to choose a favorite world beat performer to study, write about, and prepare for presentation to the class. This exercise can enhance their skills in research, writing, and oral delivery.

3. Challenge students to examine the evolution of particular world beat genres, such as Chimurenge (Shona, Zimbabwe), Bhangra (Indian-Pakistani, UK), Zouk (Haiti), Soca (Trinidad), and Pop-Rai (Algeria), with regard to their relationship to political positions and movements.

4. In a purely creative exercise, but one that explores the elements of audio recording and sound engineering (as well as composition and improvisation), guide students to seeking out traditional music that they can adapt, arrange, and use to launch into their own personal expressions. For example, recommend that they select a traditional or folk tune (see other lessons in this book for example), learn it "as written," and then arrange in a world beat way. Students may wish to add guitars, drum set, keyboard, other percussion, microphones and amplification, and techniques available in a sound studio to embellish, enhance, or distort natural sounds. The challenge, however, is in retaining some elements of the musical tradition even as innovative expressions are explored, by raising the question: What is still traditional about your world beat music?

## NOTE

1. Download a map of the world from *National Geographic* (www.nationalgeographic.com/xpeditions/atlas/) and project it on a screen for the students.

## BIBLIOGRAPHY

Broughton, Simon, Mark Ellingham, and Jon Lusk, eds. *The Rough Guide to World Music*. London: Rough Guides, 2006. This book offers what is probably the most comprehensive survey of world beat for general-interest readers.

Campbell, Patricia Shehan. *Tunes and Grooves for Music Education*. Upper Saddle River, N.J.: Pearson, 2008. A collection of notated melodies and rhythms, with cultural contexts and suggested experiences.

Diamond, Beverly. *Native American Music in Eastern North America*. New York: Oxford University Press, 2008. This book and CD set explores the contemporary musical landscape of indigenous North Americans, including the Inuit of the far north. Instructional suggestions for classroom use are found on the associated Global Music Series website.

Hast, Dorothea E., and Stanley Scott. *Music in Ireland*. New York: Oxford University Press, 2004. The authors use text and recordings to convey performance style, repertoire, and instrumentation of Irish music in Ireland and Irish America. The Global Music Series contains instructional suggestions for classroom use.

Manuel, Peter. *Popular Musics of the Non-Western World: An Introductory Survey*. Oxford: Oxford University Press, 1990. This unique scholarly book provides detailed discussion of popular music from various parts of the world.

Taylor, Timothy D. *Global Pop: World Music, World Markets*. New York: Routledge, 1997. This book discusses the music industry and the development of world beat, with detailed description of many prominent musicians.

### Internet Resources

Born to Groove, http://borntogroove.org/
Cultural Diversity in Music Education (CDIME), www.cdime-network.com/cdime
World Music Central, http://worldmusiccentral.org/

# Glossary

*Note:* The phonetic transcriptions in this glossary use the symbols listed in *Webster's New Collegiate Dictionary* (Springfield, Mass. G.-C. Merriam, 1977). The transcriptions are meant as a guide only, they do not accurately reflect every nuance of pronunciation for every term. For example, native speakers of some of the languages included here do not use accents, but elongate certain vowels.

**acculturation:** culture change that results from contact and interaction between two cultural traditions; an equivalent term is transculturation

**aerophone:** the category of instruments in which the sound is produced by activating a moving, vibrating column of air

**alphorn** \ˈalp-horn\: a long, wooden wind instrument used by herdsmen in the Alps for signaling and playing simple melodies

**anacrusis** \a-na-ˈkru-sis\: upbeat

**Andalusian cadence:** a type of ending for music that shows Spanish influence; consists of the chord progression A minor, G, F, and E (when the music is in A minor); may reflect ancient Moorish (Arabic) roots of Spanish music

**Apache violin:** the only indigenous stringed instrument among Native Americans, the Apache violin is made from a section of stalk from the century plant (a type of agave); tone holes are carved at appropriate points and one or two strings are placed lengthwise across the top of the instrument

**ballad:** a narrative song, usually handed down orally, that tells a story; also a slow jazz piece, often with a romantic theme

**bandurria** \ban-ˈdu-re-a\: Spanish lute, like a guitar but with six double courses of strings

**bass line:** usually played on a bass guitar or string bass (or sometimes on a keyboard), this consists of the lowest pitches that provide the harmonic and rhythmic foundation for a song in jazz or rock genres

**bear's roar:** a friction drum that, when played, imitates the growl of a bear

**bel canto:** a traditional European style of full voice singing, as encountered in opera

**binary structure:** a two-part structure such as a verse-chorus or A-B structure

**bitonic:** a musical scale that has only two notes

**bluegrass music:** a type of country music that is performed by singers with acoustic stringed instruments including the guitar, fiddle, banjo, mandolin, Hawaiian steel guitar (Dobro), and double bass

**bouzouki** \ba-ˈzu-ke\: a Greek long-necked lute, popular in dance ensembles

**branco** \ˈbra-ko\: the Portuguese term for "white," in this case a person with white skin; or in Brazil, a person who has been socially accepted as being economically "white" regardless of skin color

**branle** \ˈbran-al\: a traditional French dance in duple meter, dating from the fifteenth century

**bullroarer:** a musical instrument, made from a slat of wood with holes cut into it, that is tied to a string and swung through the air to produce whistle-like sounds; used by Native Americans and other cultures

**call-and-response:** a musical form that features a lead singer who sings a short phrase that is answered by a chorus or small group of singers; also applies to instrumental music when one instrument is answered by several

**canonic technique:** a compositional device in which a single melody or musical layer is repeated, starting at different times, to create a layered musical work

**cante jondo** \\'kan-ta 'hon-do\\: literally "deep song," this was the predominant vocal musical form of the Spanish gypsies and others in Andalusia, Spain; developed into the Spanish flamenco

**Cariban:** the language of the Carib Native Americans who inhabit parts of northern South America, and who were the predominant cultural group of Native Americans in the Caribbean when Columbus arrived

**castanets** \\kas-ta-'nets\\: a Spanish clapper instrument consisting of two wooden pieces tied together with a string that passes over the player's thumb and first finger; played by flamenco dancers

**Celtic harp** \\'kel-tik harp\\: the national instrument of Ireland; smaller than the orchestral harp

**ceremonial song:** song to accompany certain ancient rituals of birth, adolescence, marriage, and death

**cimbalum** \\'sim-bu-lum\\: the hammered dulcimer of Hungary

**clog:** a heavy shoe that has a thick sole; clog dancing, a dance step traditionally used in the Southern Appalachians, is a flat-footed walk with embellishments

**concertina:** a small accordion popular in Britain and France

**conjunct motion:** melodic motion by step

**coyote tales:** Native American stories with a moral, used for entertainment and for teaching right and wrong

**czardas** \\'char-das\\: Hungarian national dance in duple meter, performed in circles and by partners

**diatonic:** not chromatic; diatonic modes use a fixed pattern (traditional in Western music) of intervals

**disjunct motion:** melodic movement in skips

**dulcimer** \\'dul-si-mar\\: a plucked zither that consists of an elongated sound box with three or four strings that sound a melody and drone; traditional in the Southern Appalachian Mountains

**electrophones:** the category of instruments in which the sound is produced and transmitted or modified by electric or electronic circuitry

**epic:** a long, narrative song

**fandango** \\fan-'dan-go\\: a Spanish dance for couples, in moderate to quick triple time, accompanied by guitar and castanets

**flamenco** \\fla-'men-ko\\: a southern Spanish (Andalusian) dance, with accompanying music that includes guitar and singer and uses ornamented melodies

**flauta** \\fla-'u-ta\\: the Spanish term for flute, one of the featured solo instruments in salsa

**flipper-dinger:** a folk toy, made of a hollow reed with a cup attached at one end, that has a lightweight ball in it; when air is blown into the reed, the ball in the cup rises into the air

**friction drum:** a membranophone in which the sound is produced by rubbing the stretched drum with the fingers or other material or by stroking a stick or string that has been fixed to the drumhead, causing it to vibrate

**funky:** music played in an extremely rhythmic, strongly articulated, and danceable style

**gaida** \\' gl-da\\: bagpipe from Eastern Europe

**gee-haw-whimmy diddle:** a folk toy, similar to a top, that can spin clockwise or counterclockwise

**groove:** a very compelling and "danceable" beat formed through rhythmically precise performance

**güiro** \\'we-ro\\: a scraper used in the Caribbean and made from either a gourd (the term originally means "gourd") or metal; an important instrument in salsa and other Caribbean musics, and is perhaps derived from a Native American instrument

**hambo** \\'hahm-bo\\: a dance for couples, in triple meter, from Sweden

**heterophony:** simultaneous use of slightly different versions of the same melody by two or more performers

**hocket technique:** a compositional device in which each musical layer consists of a single sound or a sound pattern that alternates with sounds or sound patterns of other layers—each layer resting while the other is sounded

**homophony:** the multivoiced music texture in which one voice acts as the principal melody and the other voices move in the same or in a similar rhythm

**hornpipe:** a duple-metered dance of the British Isles, consisting of two groups of four eighth notes

**idiophone:** the category of instruments in which the sound is produced by the vibration of the primary material from which the instrument is made (e.g., the struck key of a marimba)

**interlocking parts:** music that is made up of several melodic parts that alternate or interlock to form a single melody; a technique used by handbell ringers in America and *siku* players in Peru and Bolivia as well as Indonesian gamelan musicians

**jig:** a dance form of the British Isles, particularly Ireland, in compound duple or triple meter

**jota** \\'ho-ta\\: a common song and dance form in Spain that features colonial rhythm

**kantele** \\'kan-tel\\: a small Finnish zither, similar to the psaltery, shaped like a bird's wing and strung with twenty to thirty strings

**katsima** \\ka-'tche-ma\\: the ancestral spirits of the Hopi or Zuni Indians of the southwestern United States; the masks or dolls made to personify or represent those spirits

**langeliek** \'lang-e-hk\: a Norwegian plucked dulcimer

**limberjack:** a rhythm instrument native to the Southern Appalachian Mountains

**loop:** common in electronic dance music and hip-hop, this consists of a sound sample that is repeated many times, sometimes serving as the basis for all or part of a song

**membranophone:** the category of instruments in which the sound is produced by the vibration of a stretched membrane, which is struck, rubbed, or otherwise activated

**microtonal:** music that is based on a system in which the pitches are spaced more closely than the Western semitone

**mode:** on its most abstract level, a series of notes arranged in scalar fashion, with a distinctive intervallic structure

**monody:** the music texture in which only one melody is sounded at a time

**mordent:** a short trill downward from the principal note

**narrative song:** a song that tells a story, such as the ballad or epic

**noter:** a narrow piece of dowel, approximately four inches long, that is placed on the melody string of a dulcimer (to the left of a selected fret) and used to change the pitch

**nykelharpa** \'nik-al-harp-a\: a keyed Scandinavian fiddle that was used for popular dance and festive music; often boat-shaped, with drone strings, one or two melody strings, and up to twelve wooden keys

**ostinato:** a musical phrase or pattern that is repeated many times; its use in salsa is derived from African music practices

**pentatonic:** any five-note scale

**play-party games:** children's songs that combined music with prescribed movement; because selection of partners was the primary function of the songs, they often provided recreational and social activities for young, rural adults

**polka:** a Polish dance in a fast duple meter

**polska** \'pols-ka\: a Swedish dance in triple meter, probably of Polish origin, similar to the mazurka

**polymeter:** the simultaneous performance of musical passages in two or more meters

**polyphony:** the music texture in which two or more rhythmically independent melodies are combined

**polyrhythm:** simultaneously sounded combinations of different rhythms that form a more or less complex rhythmic texture

**power-gathering emblem:** an object or symbol that represents or influences the political power of a ruler or ruling group

**powwow:** a contemporary gathering place for all Native Peoples to celebrate their identity and to promote Native culture; these gatherings also provide a forum for discussions of Native rights, health and educational concerns, and other sociopolitical issues, with music and dance being the centerpieces of these occasions

**pueblo** \'puab-lo\: Native American housing complex built of adobe (sun-dried mud brick), for up to several hundred people

**rachenitsa** \ra-chen-'et-sa\: the Bulgarian national dance in 7/8 meter with three beats arranged short-short-long

**rap:** highly rhythmic recitation of poetic words, usually to musical accompaniment

**reel:** a dance form of northern Europe for lines of couples, with music in duple meter

**reverse rondo form:** a form akin to the rondo except that the refrain comes after the first verse: A—Refrain—B—Refrain—C—Refrain—Refrain

**rommel pot** \'rom-mal pot\: a friction drum of the Netherlands, played by pulling a rope through a small hole in a pot

**sardana** \sar-'da-na\: a Basque circle dance in duple meter; found in southern France and the Spanish Catalan region

**schuplattler** \'shu-plat-lar\: an Austrian boot-slapping dance in triple meter

**strophic melodic structure:** a melodic structure in which the same music or melodic material is used despite changes in the text

**syncopation:** a displacement of the normal metric accent; the accentuation of normally unaccented beats

**tambur** \'tam-bur\: a long-necked, plucked lute of the Middle East and Yugoslavia

**tamburitza** \tam-bur-'it-za\: an ensemble of tamburs of different sizes and pitch ranges

**tarantella** \ta-ran-'te- la\: Italian (Neopolitan) dance in a quick 6 meter, named for the tarantula spider, whose poisonous bite the dance was supposed to cure

**tetrachord:** a series of four notes with an idiosyncratic interval structure; used in Middle Eastern music to construct modes

**tetratonic:** a four-toned scale

**timbales** \tem-'ba-las\: a Spanish term for two single-headed, shallow-bodied drums in Caribbean salsa; they are placed on stands and played by one musician

**tonal language:** a language in which meaning is determined not only by words themselves, but also by the pitches and rhythmic articulations of those words

**tritonic:** a three-toned scale

**tsamiko** \sa-me-ko\: a Greek line dance in slow 8 meter (here grouped in steps alternating slow-quick, slow-quick)

**vals** \vals\: a Scandinavian waltz, or triple-meter dance

**vamp:** repeated playing of harmonic motif (usually just one or two chords), as part of a groove; often keyboardists or rhythm guitarists will play a vamp, especially at the very beginning or end of a song

**vocable:** syllables with extra-linguistic meaning, such as *he, ne, yo,* or *heyo,* used by Native Americans to communicate special messages in their songs

**wayno** \ˈwʌy-no\: an Andean Native American dance and song form (also spelled *huayno*)

**work song:** any type of song that accompanies work or that may be used to make work easier or more efficient; often using rhythms that imitate the type of work being done

**yodlers** \ˈyod-lurz\: an Alpine song style that features frequent and rapid passing from a low chest voice to a high falsetto

# Index

# Contributors

## EDITORS

**William M. Anderson** is professor emeritus at Kent State University, where he was the founding director of the Center for the Study of World Musics. He has been president of the Ohio Music Education Association, director of the 1990 Washington MENC national symposium on "Multicultural Approaches to Music Education," chair of the Editorial Committee of the Music Educators Journal, and author and editor of a number of books including *Making Connections: Multicultural Music and the National Standards* (with Marvelene Moore) and *Integrating Music into the Elementary Classroom* (with Joy Lawrence, 8th ed.).

**Patricia Shehan Campbell** is Donald E. Peterson Professor of Music at the University of Washington. She is the author of *Musician and Teacher: Orientation to Music Education, Tunes and Grooves in Music Education, Teaching Music Globally* (and coeditor of Oxford's Global Music Series), *Songs in Their Heads*, and *Lessons from the World*, along with numerous other publications on music for children and teaching world music cultures. Her training is in Dalcroze Eurhythmics, as well as in piano and vocal performance, with specialized study in the vocal traditions of Bulgaria, India, and Pakistan. She serves on the advisory board for Smithsonian Folkways, and on various journal boards.

## CONTRIBUTORS

**Bryan Burton** is professor and chairperson of music education and coordinator of graduate studies at West Chester University. He has written and contributed to numerous books and classroom series in the field of world music education and is a frequent presenter at state, national, and international music education conferences. At present, he serves on the Editorial Board for the *International Journal of Music Education-Practice* and is a contributing editor for the *New Grove Dictionary of American Music*.

**Ann Clements**, Ph.D., is an associate professor of music education at the Pennsylvania State University School of Music. Her primary areas of interest include secondary general music, middle school/junior high choral music, music participation, and ethnomusicology, particularly within the Pacific Rim and Polynesia.

**Peter Dunbar-Hall** teaches in the Music Education Unit of the Sydney Conservatorium of Music (University of Sydney). His research interests include Australian Aboriginal music, popular music studies, history and philosophy of music education, and Balinese music and dance.

**Kay Edwards** is a professor at Miami University (Oxford, Ohio), where she teaches courses in preK–12 general and multicultural music, supervises student teachers, and directs Orff-Schulwerk workshops. Previously a music teacher in Arizona for ten years, she received grants to work with Native American artists-in-residence, and shares her materials for these musics through articles, textbooks, and numerous presentations.

**David G. Hebert** is associate professor of music education at the University of Southern Mississippi. He previously held positions with the Sibelius Academy, Boston University, Te Wananga O Aotearoa, Tokyo Gakugei University, and Moscow State University. His research interests include issues of pluralism, identity, and cultural relevance in music education.

**Ellen McCullough-Brabson**, University of New Mexico professor emerita of music education and regents' lecturer, is a multicultural music specialist. She is coauthor of *Roots and Branches: A Legacy of Multicultural Music for Children* and *We'll Be in Your Mountains, We'll Be in Your Songs: A Navajo Woman Sings*. Ellen is a coauthor of the Macmillan/McGraw-Hill music series, Spotlight on Music.

**Sarah Watts** is an instructor of music education at Bucknell University. She specializes in elementary music teaching and her research interests include transgenerational musical play, children's musical cultures, issues of musical identity, and community influences in music teaching.